Once Upon a Tom

Tales of Science, Synchrotrons & Stupidity

Mainly Stupidity

Herman, I want to know when you OPEN UP Africa. Loved Sharing SSRL with you. Tom

John A Pople

Front Cover Photo: © 2009 Jen Hostetler Photography. Used with permission
Front Cover Design: Melissa Hill
Editor: Julia Tetrud

Contact the author: madenglishscientist@yahoo.com

Even in literature and art, no man who bothers about originality will ever be original; whereas if you simply try to tell the truth (without caring twopence how often it has been told before) you will, nine times out of ten, become original without ever having noticed it

C. S. Lewis

For Tom...
...and for everyone

Contents

"I couldn't live with him,
but he's fun to watch!"

Tom's first wife

First...

The Man, The Myth[*]

Figure α.1: Thomas E Hostetler,
a.k.a. "Thomas H" a.k.a. "The Hat"
a.k.a. "*No mas! Tomas!*"

Meet Tom. Graduated philosopher (Stanford '69), former nuclear submarine electrical plant operator, former cowboy, father of three highly independent children, self-professed hippy, Buddhist and Christian; practicing Freemason chaplain and Zen-lodge member; some or all of which since 25th Jan 1942, when the wild ride began. It's a heady mix. Tom has just completed his tour of duty as a synchrotron beamline operator and x-ray technician at the Stanford Synchrotron Radiation Lightsource (SSRL).

And the Hat and pipe are fixtures.

Tom has always maintained a childlike fascination with the universe: he is genuinely intrigued by everything. The almond may have blossomed relatively early for Tom; he was white-haired when I first met him at 56, but any other trait of age is yet to appear. For the longest time, Tom was the man for whom the word "spry" was invented. Coupled with his generous nature, he would spring beneath your car at the first hint of an unusual sound. I'm not saying it would necessarily be wise for you to have

---

[*] -take?

him under there, mind you, but under there in a flash he would certainly be. Mentally, he retains that energetic exuberance and innocent wonder by which the world is experienced most deeply. Now in his seventies, Tom is the oldest teenager I know.

Tom dresses for functionality; he pays no dues to fashion's vanity, and thus the consequences can realize a novel assemblage of colors and textures. He is a walking desk drawer: generously festooned with pens, paperclips and post-it notes; stationery boutonnieres sprouting from every seam. Notes are constantly squirreled away about his person, a mix of random to-do items and fact-ettes of delight. Almost none of these survive to serve their purpose, however; they are constantly fluttering away in the disheveled autumn of Tom's breezy stride; or lost as he deposits a note-filled shirt somewhere, not to retrieve it for days. Basically, Tom looks like he has been covered head to toe in glue and pulled backwards at high speed through OfficeMax.[1]

Tom is, for my money, a natural genius. His status as a philosopher forms an apt summary *per se*, for I know no-one who has more 'philo' (love) for 'sophia' (wisdom) than Tom. Many of his observations are total nonsense, but such is the nature of the intellectual entrepreneur; and Tom seeks understanding voraciously. He will spew gibberish left and right but, just when you think he's about to start dribbling, he'll pull a blinding insight from nowhere. It might be about the physical world, etymological world, spiritual or philosophical world. No-one else I know

---

[1] But that is not to say he is a lost cause. Provided advice is sufficiently focused, Tom can be guided even on the intricacies of haberdashery. I think of the time he arrived for work in shoes styled the same as those in a bowling alley and several sizes too large; such that the slap-slap of his approach was audible long before he hove into view. Our co-worker Dave Day fixed him with a steely stare, of the type most of us reserve for pets who have defecated on priceless furniture, and, never a man to mince words, offered Tom the undecorated counseling: "You look like a ******* clown." We never did see those shoes again.

would have intuited that 'infant' and 'infantry' are connected through the common feature of being unable to speak: a baby being *physically* unable to speak and the lowest-ranked soldiers being *legally* unable to answer back. His moral observation: "Laws are for people who don't love each other enough" is exemplary, irrefutable, wisdom; unconsciously espousing the teaching of Jesus of Nazareth. And who, while watching tennis, discerns: "There's no reason to score '30-all': it's identical to deuce"? He's absolutely right. One of the best-known sports in the world has a scoring system which contains a genuine mathematical redundancy. If the umpire were to call "deuce" at 30-all, and call play thereafter as so, not a single result from history would change. I wonder how many, even in London's proud SW19 at the All-England Lawn Tennis and Croquet Club (a.k.a. Wimbledon), have deduced this? Precious few, I fancy.

Tom solved the riddle I created especially for him:

"Who hast altered most red?"
"We that stored shame, Lord."

He figured out that the letters of question and answer are exact anagrams of each other and – *le coup de grace* – an anagram of his own name: Thomas Edward Hostetler. It took him a while, but he did not have to be told.

This hunger for learning produces Tom's inconvenient bouts of intellectual rigor. Woe betide the lazy scientist who tries to brush him off with a hand-waving bluff; as I discovered to my cost. On the day he was probing for a better understanding of the nano-scale interaction between partially polarized water molecules, even allowing that my belabored brain was in a state of delicacy from our previous evening's refreshments, my weak postulate: "Just Google it" was treated with the derisive scorn which, on reflection, it merited.

While Tom's vigorous curiosity is certainly impressive, it is equally important you understand Tom's generosity. In charitable provision the man is peerless: many a self-professed Christian is called to look to his laurels. No beggar will go conveniently unnoticed, no hitchhiker passed by, no fellow human unassisted where assistance is wont. Tom may yet call St Francis of Assisi to account to ask why the man was so silly as to only be useful to animals.

Tom's generosity is not limited to those who beg for it, either. Here's an unusual example – and with Tom, there can be no other type, as you will ultimately discover. In the early days of SSRL, where we worked, Tom learned that the Idaho Lead Bank was shutting down and dispensing 80 tons of lead for free – including free delivery. Tom knew that SSRL needed lead for shielding the gamma rays which are generated whenever it runs. He claimed the bounty and, realizing that the lead would arrive in portions too large for human manipulation, bargained with an organization in Washington state to have it cut into manageable bricks (8 x 4 x 2 inches; 26 lbs a piece) paying for the service with a quarter of the source material. The bottom line: SSRL received 60 tons of lead, formed into several thousand bricks of manageable magnitude, for free. They're in use today, all $100 000 worth, shielding gamma rays on every beamline in the synchrotron. Tom's remuneration? Nothing. The lab evidently never thought to offer him anything and, superbly, Tom never needed to ask. He had the internal satisfaction of being genuinely useful, for Tom a payment finer than gold. To this day, the vast majority of the lab's staff has no idea where these bricks originated (humorously including those who hoard them rather possessively). Nor does Tom need them to know.

Tom is supremely environmentally conscious, too; making every effort to leave only the lightest footfalls on our delightful, delicate, planet home. But here is where his haphazard organizational capabilities impede his noble intent. A simple

5

example: if Tom determines he needs only five pages printed from a 200-page document, he will exert himself to make it so. But there's still an infinitely greater likelihood of him unwittingly entering the number "5" in the "No. of Copies" field than anywhere else. Minutes later he will be found in the mail room, arms akimbo in dismay, as the printer merrily machine-guns a thousand pages all over the floor. Tom will try to stem the flow of waste, but no more successfully than the kitten who is perennially trying to catch the laser dot, and equally as baffled. Finally he will cast his hands skyward in an (unheard) appeal for mercy and stand motionless, gaping at the disaster, only to complain in a voice of wounded innocence to any who will listen about how the computer has got it all terribly wrong again.[2]

Despite this, or perhaps for intention alone, Tom secured an Environmental Stewardship Champion award. Yet even here irony abounds, as the award lies amidst more hazardous trash than could ever have been cleaned up to earn it (Figure α.2).

Thus there is no doubt in my mind that Tom is both a genuine genius and an equally genuine philanthropist; many a tale will attest to these assertions. This book, however, does not necessarily center on those tales...

---

[2] It is perfectly ironic that as I type these words, I see some printing from Hostetler's earlier shift here on the beamline operator's desk. Evidently Tom has been tasked to produce Caution signs for radioactive experiments on the beamlines. International convention insists these signs be yellow and black, so the fact he's used the black and white printer to produce sad gray shadows of what's required does not put him away to a winning start. But what takes the cake is that he's somehow managed to waste many sheets inadvertently printing the email header to which the single color example was attached. How does he do it? I sincerely hope no-one asks him to do it again properly. Trees without number will plummet spiraling to their doom as Tom pokes hopefully at the keyboard again and again; the majestic Stanislaus forest will shrink to a mere copse before our very eyes.

Figure α.2: Tom's Environmental Stewardship Champion award, languishing amidst his office detritus. The substance in the bottom left on the vacuum bellows is unknown, and may conceivably be a new element

But it is essential for you to know about Tom's piercingly keen intellect and true heart because it provides the occasional explanation, but usually the mind-boggling counter-point, for what follows. You will encounter the 'Tom Story' in all its manifold glorious incarnations. Typically each incident consists of Tom's ingenuity and generosity in full flow, if slightly misdirected, coupled with an amount of chutzpah that would usually land a man in jail. Together, Tom's brilliance and the forensic details of each anecdote form the perfectly imperfect contradiction that is Life with Tom. You will sample, if only vicariously, the heartfelt appreciation, and limb-chewing frustration, of a shared existence.

As the phrase our co-worker, the late Bill Butler, immortalized: "Working with Tom is like a box of chocolates. Never know what you're going to get."

Please fasten your seat-belt.

Co-Starring

Joe Leonard Dave Day Tom Hostetler

Tim Dunn Joe Tocci John Pople

Figure α.3: 2014 SSRL Beamline Operators (not including the elephant)

Bill Butler (1948-2011) JR Troxel Bethany Lyles
2001 intern

Bart Johnson Jenny Hostetler Emily Hostetler

Figure α.4: Family and SSRL co-workers contributing to this book

9

Setting the Scene

Many Tales of Tom are based at his longtime place of employ: the SLAC National Accelerator Laboratory,[3] where Tom worked for a staggering 46 years (or 1.5 billion seconds, as Tom would likely prefer it recorded); myself alongside him for his last seventeen.

SLAC is a particle accelerator: essentially a machine which uses timed radio frequency pulses and magnetic steering to accelerate sub-atomic particles, in this case electrons and positrons, close to the (theoretically unachievable) speed of light in evacuated tubes in order to crash them headlong into each

Figure α.5: 2014 was Tom's 46th and final year at SSRL, SLAC

other to see what's inside, or if anything interesting happens, such as the whole lab going up in smoke. This is the world of high energy physics, whose signature achievement, overlooking the awkward elephant in the room, the hydrogen bomb, is a vast

---

[3] It is said a camel is a horse designed by committee, and this hopeless hybrid name has a similarly tortured genesis. Since time immemorial (1962 to be more accurate) SLAC stood for: 'Stanford Linear Accelerator Center.' But in 2008 the US government's Department of Energy acquired the laboratory and needed to remove the name 'Stanford,' for bureaucratic reasons which I neither know nor care about. After power-struggles, tantrums and probably some chair-throwing with those who were as emotionally fused *to* the Stanford name as those opposed, the compromise was that 'SLAC' would remain as a word, not an acronym. (Those with the misfortune to have experienced an acrimonious divorce and are left clinging white-knuckled to their mangled half of a now wholly inoperable toaster will have a good feeling for how this process works.) Thus 'SLAC' is now alleged to be a word (hopeless!) to avoid having the acronym 'SLACNAL,' where 'Accelerator' would appear twice (also hopeless). The compromise? 'SLAC National Accelerator Laboratory' (utterly hopeless): our very own etymological camel.

array of baffling terminology, presumably to keep the uninitiated from discovering that it's little more than grown-up kids bashing their toys together for giggles, while asking for jaw-dropping sums of money to be able to do so.

SLAC has a long and illustrious history: several Nobel prizes have been won here; all of which is detailed elsewhere. For the more casual observer, one may simply enjoy that it's the longest building in North America, at a smidge over three kilometers, and the third longest building in the world, after the Great Wall of China and some fortress in Pakistan I'd never heard of until I looked this up.[4] If you're flying in to California's San Francisco or San Jose airport, peer out of the window and you may readily see it (Figure α.6).

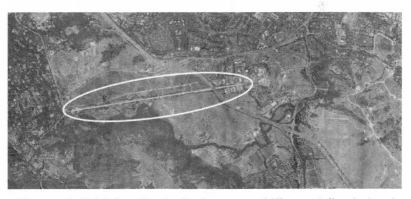

Figure α.6: SLAC from the air: the above-ground Klystron gallery is ringed

SLAC needs to be straight and level to the nth degree, so building it in Silicon Valley, where the ground is as prone to fluctuations as the stock market, may seem a cretinous choice. But the ability to lie sprawled on Capitola beach, frost-glistened margarita in hand, listening to the soft roar of the Pacific, in less than an hour from leaving the lab provides ample justification for the location, in my expert opinion. Besides, the juddering earth beneath the precision-aligned accelerator is neatly countered by

---

[4] http://en.wikipedia.org/wiki/List_of_longest_buildings_in_the_world

the 1970s construction of the Interstate 280 overpass which shakes it from above as well (Figure α.6). And in reality there is a plethora of motorized gizmos which constantly sense movement and apply the necessary real-time tweaks to keep the accelerator straight, even while California squirms around as if it has an itch.

A fascinating feature of the SLAC linear accelerator building is that it's too long to be able to see the end when inside the gallery. One can look directly at the end wall, which does not go around a corner or over a rise, but is just too far away for the human eye to resolve in detail (Figure α.7).

SLAC's early success spawned further particle accelerators on the same site. The early 70's gave rise to what is now SSRL: the Stanford Synchrotron Radiation Lightsource.[5] A third accelerator launched in 2009: the Linear Coherent Light Source (LCLS)[6] the world's most powerful x-ray laser and first x-ray free electron laser. LCLS' primary novel ability is to 'see' molecular motion in real time during interactions; the pulsed laser has sufficient brilliance to detect a single molecule in motion. In a satisfying circle-of-life twist, LCLS makes use of much of the original SLAC accelerator, on which experimentation was in decline.

---

[5] More camels, alas, and from the same debacle that inspired SLAC's new butchered moniker. SSRL, formerly: 'Stanford Synchrotron Radiation Laboratory' was renamed: 'Stanford Synchrotron Radiation Lightsource' in 2008. There's no such word as 'Lightsource,' as anyone with an IQ above room-temperature knows, but the scientists are frequently at the mercy of bureaucratic nonsense. Or perhaps it was just that no-one could be bothered to change all the SSRL-emblazoned stationery.

[6] The correct use of "Light Source" as two words in the LCLS acronym forms both a direct contradiction to, and screaming indictment of, the stupidity of the word "Lightsource" in the current SSRL acronym. But we all pretend not to notice, to be polite to the management. Besides, LCLS will very likely be renamed the 'Lovelyandstraight Coherent Lightscience Sciencething' at the next review anyway.

Figure α.7: SLAC Klystron gallery interior, looking West over 1.5 miles

Thus, there are three particle accelerators on the Stanford site: two straight accelerators (SLAC & LCLS) and a circular one (SSRL) where Tom works. The purpose of SSRL is to generate x-rays to be able to 'see' at the molecular level. SSRL produces x-rays by spinning sub-atomic particles (electrons) around a ring of ~80 meters diameter at close to the speed of light. The electrons get so hot they radiate x-rays and, while the electrons are held in their orbit by magnets, the x-rays fly off down straight tubes extending tangentially from the ring like the legs on a spider (beamlines) into lead-lined rooms where the experiments take place. The lead-lined rooms are called "hutches" because the first such 'room' where these x-rays were used was an old rabbit hutch.[7] Sample materials, either biological or synthetic, are probed by the beams and the resulting scattered x-ray patterns unlock secrets within the world of nano-scale science: the molecular scale. Nano-scale research is booming because the molecular scale, while neither the smallest nor largest scale we can explore, seems to be the busiest and most influential in organic and synthetic processes. It may not be too much of a simplification to say that life, in all its complexity, happens more at the molecular level than any other.

Scientific discovery occurs as much by accident as by design; the distribution of research buildings on the SLAC site reflects this. Buildings spring up to casually invade the sky wherever they are needed. Some sit alone in deep hollows far removed from all else, as if sulking or rejected, with deer tramping undisturbed around them. Others pile on top of each other as if for shared warmth, like the sea-lions at Pier 39. The configuration of buildings at SSRL has the latter appearance.

I enjoy the priorities at play: science takes precedence over architecture. If a major experiment won't fit in the building, walls are knocked down so it will. An exterior wall of SSRL's main synchrotron building was shoved outwards several meters to incorporate a new hutch for a giant 13 Tesla magnet and, as a result, a stairway which used to be outside is now caught in a weird limbo state in an outdoor corridor, while interior space swarms around it. I've worked at eleven synchrotron and

---

[7] I. Lindau, P. Pianetta, S. Doniach and W.E. Spicer, Nature 1974, Vol. 250, pp 214 - 215

spallation facilities in five countries and I'm well aware that this readiness to butcher buildings for the precedence of science is rare. But it does neatly capture the pioneering spirit of America's West coast.

Tom worked in SSRL most recently as a Beamline Operator: an overseer of all 30 experimental stations at the branched ends of all the dozen or so beamlines. The beamline operator's job is to provide immediate support, to the best of his abilities, in case of any malfunction of the beamline: optical, electrical, vacuum or electronic; as well as offering software and scientific support where possible. The post is manned 24/7 for the nine months a year the synchrotron runs, by one of a team of operators who carry a set of master keys and a cellphone which fields the emergency calls.[8]

But more relevant to Tom's life than his employment circumstances is his outlook upon said venture. Tom sails his life's vessel solely within the currents of enjoyment and enthusiastically invites any and all to join him therein. (In the SSRL environment, to its own credit, this is eminently achievable.) Say to Tom: "Have fun!" and I guarantee he will respond: "I know how!" You'll notice that, I warrant, in what follows...

---

[8] The cellphone fields the calls significantly better when it isn't dropped down the SSRL kitchen's garbage disposal unit, however, as Tom ably demonstrated in Jun 2014. Perhaps this was his novel way to delete voicemail? This is unclear. Either way, we had to get another one.

Theirs not to make reply,
Theirs not to reason why,
Theirs but to do and die:
Into the valley of Death
Rode the six hundred.
"The Charge of the Light Brigade," Lord Tennyson

Chapter 1:
Working with Tom

The Wake

We won't get far without introducing The Wake. The Wake is the signature trail of destruction that streams out behind Tom's less judicious life-choices. Most commonly, by the time the blunder's consequences descend Tom has left the scene, with a timing exquisite enough to make a ballet troupe weep, leaving a smorgasbord of co-workers and bystanders bobbing helplessly in the aftermath. After seventeen years' schooling in surfing The Wake, I am reasonably adept at navigating its swells and riptides, but in truth, any one of Tom's most experienced co-workers – all Wake-surfers *extraordinaire* – can be pitched into the drink at any moment, ever-grateful for whatever ankle-leashes of ingenuity still shackle us to the surfboard of employment.

As always, this is best viewed by example.

One summer day, Tom is the scheduled beamline operator, with SSRL's master keys and the cellphone taking emergency calls forwarded from the control station landline. It's August, and the local Alpine Inn's pub garden inveigles us once more into her steamy embrace. Tom inhales a couple of beers at the speed most of us would only drink on Doomsday and spontaneously decides to take the next two days off (in the same way a ship's captain might step onto an island mid-cruise and say: "Forget this captaincy malarkey, I'm stopping here"). Tom asks co-worker Joe Tocci, sat next to him, to stand in as cover. Joe replies he is out on medical the next day, and so can't. Tom, not listening to a damn word, merrily enters Joe's name in place of his on the online schedule anyway. At day's end, Tom correctly turns the operator's cellphone off and locks it away (there's no overnight coverage in summer) but critically forgets to deactivate the call-forwarding. Thus instead of the control station landline ringing while the cell is unmanned, all emergency calls are now forwarded to a cellphone that is switched off and locked away.

And then drives home with the keys. Boom.

Next morning, as if by prescient conspiracy of the universe, the monochromator at Beamline 7-3 starts overheating. A sophisticated alarm system detects this and automatically calls the beamline operator cellphone, specifying the exact problem by preset text message. But the alarm's sophistication is no match for the all-conquering buffoonery of Hostetler. The cellphone is still off and locked away, the call-forwarding is still on, so the landline won't ring, Tocci, out on medical, is listed as the responsible operator and Tom is home in Santa Cruz, re-acquainting himself with oblivion via whatever bottles of wine, whisky or Drano are within reach.

Eventually, the systems manager Mike Horton scrambles into the lab as his phone melts down with re-forwarded calls; and I belatedly pry the cellphone out of the lockbox to sift through its various electronic shrieks of disaster. When the Sword of Damocles falls, the apparent culprit is a choice between the operator named on the schedule (Tocci) and the only operator present on scene (me); either of whom must account for how this fault – a serious one – could go so long unaddressed. Yet the whole time, as decreed by the inviolable laws of The Wake, the actual muppet responsible escapes entirely unscathed. To this day, Tom knows nothing of this story.

Behold The Wake! Marvel at its mighty powers!

Epilogue: Day's end at Santa Cruz; and a tinted sunset caresses the aqueous horizon. A man sinks gently into the rooftop hot-tub and gazes out at the ocean from the beachfront property his insurers provided after he burned his own house down (don't ask). The silhouette of The Hat stands proud and black on a pastel sky as scented pipe-smoke coils lazily into the ambience from beneath its rim. A carefree, if off-key, slurring of alcohol-infused ditties adorns the nightscape, from one blithely unaware of the carnage trailing out behind him...

Once Upon a Tom
"Trying Very Hard to be Helpful"

"The best is he who calls men to the best. And those who heed the call are also blessed. But worthless who call not, heed not, but rest."

Hesiod, ~700 BC

Tom's determination to assist is legendary. Your car is leaking an undetermined fluid? Tom is the first to hurl himself beneath it to facilitate diagnosis, even if dressed in a tuxedo. That's not to say he won't accidently hook a cufflink on your brake lines and disconnect them, inadvertently killing you and all your loved ones – but he's genuinely minded to help and frequently wise enough to know what he's doing. But if you're using his self-confidence as a first-order gauge of his expertise, take care! With Tom, no such coupling exists. His self-confidence is always at a premium; yet the relevant expertise factor can vary starkly. This is not to impugn Tom's innocence: Tom is always innocent. But so is a volcano.

More than twenty years ago a research crew from the University of California in Los Angeles (UCLA) came to SSRL to probe nano-scale devices they had synthesized to act as high-efficiency solar energy cells. On this trip, the gods of chance chose not to smile kindly. More accurately, they chose to leer. Later years revealed that the professor leading this group is thrifty in her expenditures and thus seeks, nay expects, high data yields from each experimental voyage into the northern part of the state. But for this particular trip anything that could go wrong, did go wrong. One man stood alone to help them. Tom.

Tom labored long and hard to help them, even beyond his shift, but no solution was forthcoming. Finally, it was declared a total wash-out and all retired for the night. There could be no doubt that Tom had done his utmost to solve problems, even if the more tangible results suggested he had occupied the role of saboteur. The professor could not fault Tom's heart or dedication. So when she was provided with the summary form for all departing experimenters she wrote, perhaps with teeth gritted hard enough to split steel:

"Tom tried very hard to be helpful."

This phrase was immortalized in hilarity. In the many years that have since passed it has been cast about by Tom's closest work colleagues time without number as the ultimate back-handed compliment. Little does the UCLA professor know what a significant contribution she has made to the SSRL lexicon.

For example: you will be having one of those days when everything you do fails utterly. You work tirelessly, yet haplessly, on an experimenter's treasured device (often a contraption whose very design defies common sense, though it seems churlish to say so at the time). Your efforts are demonstrably creating more problems than they're solving and then, at that very moment, a fellow staff member wanders by wearing a broad smirk. "Trying very hard to be helpful?" he or she may quip as you grit your teeth and grimace. Worse yet, bystanders are minded to compliment your grinning, evil-spirited colleague for the encouragement they appear to be offering. They likely miss the strangled pain on your reddening face as you know that deliberate insult is being added to injury, all justified in the name of humor and twisted SSRL love.

Yet naturally, no-one is on the receiving end of this timeless jibe more frequently than the man who first gave it life: once upon a Tom.

Dancing the 110V Bop

It was my first day. Mon 5th Jan 1998. I'd literally touched down in America from England only the day before.

My main purpose was to resurrect a disused beamline. As I've said, SSRL is a synchrotron source: an evacuated circular tunnel in which sub-atomic particles (electrons) are accelerated close to the speed of light. The electrons are over-energized and they radiate ever decreasing wavelengths in order to shed energy more efficiently. The radius of the synchrotron circle determines the effective 'fastest speed' of the electrons and thus the peak energy of the radiation. SSRL's 80 meter diameter 'tunes' the radiated peak energy to the x-ray region.

The electrons – the x-ray's source – always remain in the ring and beamlines are simply openings in the ring, down which the shed x-rays shoot, into the experimental hutches. The beamlines are straight because the x-rays will travel in a straight line, even though they're cast from objects traveling in a circle. This is rudimentary physics: if you spin something in a circle it gains angular momentum, yet the moment you let go it travels in a straight line, since the angular momentum is not the inherent attribute of its free motion but a consequence of a pinned constraint. One of these beamlines (Beamline 1-4) hadn't been used in a while and it was my place to re-commission it.

I'd been in the building barely an hour when Tom descended. He could obviously spot a greenhorn wandering around wide-eyed and helpless among enough electronics to provide a convincing backdrop for a Star Trek movie and, as is his nature, he sought only to help.

Early on it was clear that a motion controller: a device designed to send the appropriate stream of electrical pulses to a motor to govern torque, speed and direction, was unresponsive. The fuse was blown: a simple fix.

I unplugged the device and trotted off to find a fuse. The fuse sits in a metal canister with a sharp nipple at the far end. Ideally for safety, the nipple is the live contact and the canister is the neutral contact, but this home-made device was wired backwards. Of course when powered down, it won't matter. Yet as I inserted the fuse into the canister, my arm began to shake uncontrollably. I had apparently lost all dexterous control and my arm flopped around spastically. White men can't dance, but this was poor even so. Stupidly I merely tried again and again to insert the fuse, with the same result. I had no idea I was experiencing electric shock. Excuse my British snobbery, but England's electrical mains runs at 240 V and when one is connected to it there's usually a helpfully loud "Bang!" and your arm flies backwards to the point of near-dislocation to assist you to deduce your error. With the relatively wimpy US supply, I had ended up dancing the 110 V bop three or four times before finally realizing I was connected to the grid. But I'd unplugged the controller, so how could this be?

I peered around the electrical rack and saw Tom kneeling next to the socket in which the device was now reconnected. His wizened face looking up at me expectantly, with the innocence of a spaniel. "Is it working now?" he asked hopefully. It was my first day and I felt the overwhelming need to tread softly. I politely solicited Tom's cooperation in unplugging the device again while I inserted the fuse. He graciously obliged. I returned behind the rack and took a minute to fumble the fuse from my pocket once more. Back into the canister it went, and my 110 V bop instantly resumed. "How about now?" floated over the helpful voice.

I realized that if I was going to survive this job, I was going to have to scramble up the learning curve of working with Tom pretty quickly...

DC Specialist

Figure 1.1: B&Z Model 167 Cart

It could reach 35 mph. ("Zoomy!" as Tom would say.) Such was the zippiness of JR Troxel's electric cart, which he provided in the early '90s as on-site transport for SSRL's x-ray group (Tom, Dave & JR). With just one drive wheel and steered by tiller, it was the oddest of vehicles, and prone to three-wheeler speed wobbles at the top end. But in time it became very popular with the crew: they learned tricks, such as leaning it over on two wheels round corners and even pulling wheelies.

But first it needed restoration, since it was purchased in barely functional state. It was powered by 36 V in six batteries, with associated solenoids, and clearly something was failing since performance was crippled. Dave and Tom, the would-be restoration mechanics, hooked it up to a fast charger overnight to overcharge the cells to aid repair. But a faulty overcharged cell can readily effuse explosive hydrogen gas, building up as a clandestine cloud in its casing...

The batteries for the almost-toy-car are under the seat. One sunny afternoon work began in earnest: Dave is craning over the battery bank through the passenger door, Tom, directing proceedings, leaning in through the other. JR, the owner, is hovering nearby trying not to get his hands dirty. Jumper cables are being waved around in an effort to diagnose electrical shorts.

"When I say 'go,' hook these on here," Tom said authoritatively, pointing at one battery pack. Dave was dubious. "Let me at least get some safety glasses on first," he replied. "Don't worry, I'm a DC specialist!" came the fateful reassurance.

JR, by his own admission, was getting nervous and ran away. Dave donned the glasses (a decision he was never to regret) and took hold of the claw grips. "Go!" says Tom.

"The last thing I remember…" Dave recounts:

spark **"WOOOMPH!!"**

The top of the battery pack blew clean off. "I was wet and it wasn't water" Dave recalled, scowling. Even JR heard the explosion from the nearby building. He peeked out to see Dave dancing, shouting curses and heading at high speed for the emergency shower. Dave's thundered indictments, while unprintable, stridently decried the alleged qualifications of the DC specialist. He was caught between the intense desire to stay in place to complete a comprehensive rebuke of the man who had triggered his acid bath; balanced by the equally strong urge to hastily retreat to the shower to wash the scalding acid from his body.

When all was again calm, the carnage could be reviewed. The battery was obliterated. Dave's T shirt and Levis were ruined: liberally perforated by acid burns. Tellingly, there were sulphuric splashes on his safety glasses, too.

Needless to say, Tom was untouched. Behold The Wake!

Instantly the diagnostic exercises were cancelled in favour of buying new solenoids and replacing the detonated battery. The mechanical restoration crew, formerly under the glorious leadership of the man known as The Hat, was equally swiftly disbanded. And the verdict of the D.C. specialist himself?

"Wow, I didn't think that was going to happen."

Splashy, Splashy

Tom loves giving tours of the lab. He's superb at it too: his mind is a vast store of miscellanea, itself worthy of touring, but more importantly he thrives on helping other people learn and enjoy themselves.

And just one of the many fun things about the SSRL beamline floor is the abundance of liquid nitrogen (LN).

Nitrogen boils at 77 Kelvin (-196 °C) so LN is always at least that cold. Since the atomic mass is light compared to, e.g., a metal, it's not as lethal as it sounds: one can wave a hand through it more casually than through a candle flame (~900 °C) without injury; but sustained contact will leave a serious burn. At SSRL, LN is mainly used for cooling the beamline crystals that select the wavelength from the broad spectrum of x-rays illuminating them so the crystals don't physically distort. But it's also entertaining: slosh it along the floor and it will be a temporary tsunami, crackling the floor tiles and manufacturing myriad mobile dust bunnies that shiver, contort and disappear in mere seconds.

Needless to say, when Tom led a bright and bushy-tailed tour group of would-be scientists from a local college, in 2007, LN play was guaranteed to ensue. Tom invited the Bay Area's finest young minds (every one blithely unaware of The Wake, bless their innocent, unjaded hearts); to dip their fingers into the LN, frothing in the plastic cup he held. Instantly a half-dozen digits extended, as if lambs to the slaughter, and duly obeyed. (I'm just happy he didn't ask them to immerse their heads.)

The tour was covered by a San Jose Mercury News journalist and photographer, so the moment is duly captured on film and broadcast to the paper's extensive readership (Figure 1.2). The journalist was evidently talented, perfectly deducing

Tom's mood and spirit in entitling his piece: "**Students visit toy store of science**,"[1] as said toy-store feel was created entirely by the white-haired Willy Wonka at the helm.[2]

Figure 1.2: "Watch This!" *Pshhht* "Ow!" The girl far right seems to be shrinking away from the entire affair and I predict she will live longest

Let's be clear: the chances of injury are minuscule. Yet predictably, when the powers that be witnessed the picture of disposable cup, semi-disposable fingers and total absence of gloves and safety glasses, they convulsed in OSHA-induced seizures. (Personally, I'm only surprised at the absence of Hat and pipe.) Ergo, a few days later a managerial shepherd's crook appeared from stage left and yanked Tom by the neck into the wings for urgent remedial instruction.

Tom learned his lesson, too. He never took professional photographers on tour again.

---

[1] N Gonzalez, "Students visit toy store of science," San Jose Mercury News 06 Dec 2007, http://www.mercurynews.com/ci_7649057
[2] Photo: J Green, *Ibid*. Original caption: "Students, mostly from Cañada College in Redwood City, putting their fingers in liquid nitrogen as Tom Hostetler, left, a longtime worker at the Stanford Linear Accelerator Center in Menlo Park, guides the group along part of a tour."

Once Upon a Tom
"Stop it! Stop it! Stop it!"

I frequently travel internationally for a charity of which I am a Director.[3] At such times the beamline I supervised while I was a research physicist (BL1-4) required a stand-in. BL1-4 was elderly and cantankerous, with many idiosyncrasies, so matching credentials were required to handle it. Tom had no science degree but his peerless resourcefulness fitted the bill. Mostly.

Where Tom did not excel was in pandering to excessive timidity, not even from visitors. Tom does science, as he does everything, **boldly**; timidity is simply not countenanced. So when a female student from south-east Asia, a demographic that can tend toward the gentle and cautious, was experimenting on BL1-4 in my absence in 2009, with Tom as resident experimental support, it gave rise to a culture clash of cataclysmic proportions.

Ms P, as we'll call her, was using an oven I'd designed and Tom had fabricated to heat her polymer samples. The heating profile was sophisticated: it could attain 400 °C through any pre-programmed profile. But there was no cooling mechanism; one had to tediously wait for ambience to restore. Ms P impatiently told Tom that a faster cooling process should be available.

Be careful what you wish for.

Re-enter LN, ambrosia of the entertainment gods. For large quantity usage, LN is stored in 180 liter dewars at pressures up to 50 psi, and even here Tom has his own unique handling protocols (Figure 1.3). Smaller quantities are decanted into open dewars; and it was one such 15 liter dewar Tom carried, striding into the hutch, Ms P following meekly, which he dumped unceremoniously on the scalding oven, (devoid of any protective clothing, to which he is evidently psychologically allergic). The

---

[3] The Williamsburg Christadelphian Foundation: http://wcfoundation.org

28

hissing of a thousand cats blasted their ears and they were enveloped in clouds of roiling steam. (I wouldn't have been too impressed myself. While the LN is harmless *per se*, the thermal shock to the heating cores isn't, which is almost certainly why they kept failing shortly thereafter. Dammit, Hostetler.)

But for the poor girl, the unexpected blast sent her over the edge. Dave Day happened to be passing above on the mezzanine bridge and heard the unusually fierce effervescence, punctuated by high-pitched screams of: **"Stop it! Stop it! Stop it!"** from the terrified student. Immediately he knew The Hat was on deck. Dave peered over the bridge to see Ms P running from the hutch with Tom closing in hot pursuit, attempting to calm her with platitudes. Tom's efforts were impeded by the fact he was still swinging the 15 liter dewar, slopping leftover LN dribbles around as he did his morning coffee; while she dodged and cowered, looking

Figure 1.3: Tom striving to un-stick a frozen valve on a 180 litre LN dewar. He is warming it with a hairdryer (recommended) and also thumping it with a hammer (not recommended); all the while with the 50 psi relief valve staring him squarely in his unshielded schnozz (insane). Bonus points for the screwdriver (circled) loaded point-up in his waistband, aimed at his vital organs should he stumble

for new places to run away. Dave was laughing so hard he was crying, while at the same time trying not to be heard. (It's arguably of artistic merit for the entire scene to be re-enacted and set to Benny Hill music.)

Ms P didn't come back. I just hope she's not in an Asian hospital somewhere, arms round knees, rocking slowly.

Missing Body Parts

I took the shift-work role of SSRL beamline operator at the age of 43, transferring from twenty years as a research physicist. It was the first time I'd had a rigid start-time to my day since I worked shifts during University vacations (warehouseman, gas station cashier, hospital janitor, etc) back in the early '90s.

So my body was already feeling rather fragile as it was hauled from slumber and grudgingly propelled, zombie-like, onto the synchrotron bridge at 05:30 that morning in 2013 to relieve Tom, who'd worked the night shift. I'd been coddled for the last two decades with the luxury of getting up pretty much whenever I wanted; so this new practice was a rude awakening in ways both metaphorical and brutally literal. It was in this delicate state that morning, that it was there to greet me. Tom's 70 year old tooth. Right in the middle of the desk.

Do you find your morning workplace adorned with the randomly discarded body parts of your coworkers? You don't? Well, you haven't lived. Or at least, you haven't lived with Tom.

Now about that tooth: try and envisage it. Have you pictured a full-length specimen? Good. Is it a faintly off-white, porcelain colour? Ah, then here I must correct you. The tooth Tom had abandoned in the middle of the operators' communal workspace was, in fact, jet black, with portions of scary-looking ochre. At first I didn't even realize it was a tooth until a (much-regretted) closer inspection.

Of course Tom wasn't there at that precise moment, he'd stepped away. Typical; I thought, once again I've been left to paddle alone in The Wake; and a very early morning paddle at that. It was a few moments before he casually loped back into view. There was clearly a need to talk. And by talk, I mean yell.

"DAMMIT HOSTETLER!"

"Good morning!" he hallooed cheerily. It's notoriously difficult to intimidate Tom: for one thing, he simply doesn't pay enough attention.

"WHAT THE HELL IS THIS?!"
"Oh, there it is!"

"Why is your tooth in the middle of the desk?"
"Because it fell out of my head."
I suppose I asked for that.

"That tooth is *nasty* Tom, look it's black!"
"You know better." This is Tom's ultimate fall-back when attempting to rebut the screamingly obvious. It's a debating trick which tries to establish a condition where either you agree or confess inadequate knowledge. Even before six a.m., I wasn't falling for that.

"Why leave it there? Do I look like the bloody Tooth Fairy?"
laughter

"You'd make her throw up and quit her job!"
"Oh hush, lad."

"What next? Tomorrow I find your leprous leg discarded on the desk? An infected eyeball watching me balefully from the control chassis? A jaundiced kidney oozing wetly into the keyboard? For crying out loud, Hostetler, keep your body parts to yourself, can't you? Stop splattering them all over the workplace!"
"Quit your whining, boy."

Tom just blew it off. I chased him from the building with a liberal peppering of rebukes, but he was clearly unflustered. Much to my chagrin.

The Demon Bean that is Caffeine

Tom never had a problem admitting his mistakes. This remained true even if his boo-boos were considerable in either dollars or damage; and it's a wonderful testimony to Tom's easy honesty and natural humility. The rest of us hid our inadequacies as best as we were able; stashing the corpses of our mistakes in whatever caverns lent availability and sneaking off with furtive backward glances. But Tom was an open book.

Charmingly, however, his commendable conduct bore the oddest of exceptions. He would never admit spilling his coffee, despite doing so daily. His resistance in this matter was absolute. Confess to damaging a quarter-million dollar monochromator by fitting the crystals improperly? No problem. Own up to being the source of the (still wet) coffee splashes leading from the kitchen to his feet, underneath the dripping coffee mug he's holding at 45 degrees? Not a chance. He would survive *waterboarding* on this point. It was strangely endearing.

And sometimes Tom simply drank far too much coffee – an instantly recognizable condition. His countenance adopted a wild-eyed stare and his decibel level doubled: he would literally *holler* his way around the lab. If uninitiated, you would hear his cry, at a volume normally reserved for terrorist attacks, and leap from your chair to assist before learning it was merely triggered by Tom being unable to find a stapler, coupled with his being two thirds of his way down the communal pot of Joe.

One morning a partial beam loss was reported at Beamline 2-1. I was aware Tom had already had several times the amount of coffee than was good for him (not counting the portion I could see liberally adorning walls and floors) and he was zigzagging around the laboratory in a native state. I scurried to the beamline knowing I had mere moments to find the fault. This

I summarily failed to achieve and Tom descended, scattering furniture, to assume control. Within seconds he roared in a voice that could be heard in Oakland that the fault was due to the phase of the moon. (I kid you not.) In fairness, the relative placements of sun and moon can cause land tides which do affect some aspects of the synchrotron, but as a suggested cause in this case it was monumentally off-base. It would be equivalent to a doctor bursting into the Operating Room, bundling nurses out of the way, glancing once at the gurney-ridden patient and immediately bellowing for a lawnmower.

But dialoguing with a caffeinated Hostetler presented a challenge far mightier than the combats of Hellenic legend, so I rested my head, eyes half-closed, against the lead-lined hutch door and waited for the universe to restore herself. On balance, it seemed the wisest thing to do.

It took several minutes, but the synchrotron operations crew assured Tom by phone that astronomy was not to blame. I could return to the fray, while Tom continued to gibber planetary misinformation behind me. It transpired that one of the upstream slits was more closed than the software was reporting; the matter was solved and the missing x-ray beam restored. Tom's indictment of the cosmos was invalid, but he was undeterred and took off: loud, caffeinated and purposeful in a clockwise direction around the synchrotron. Heaven alone knows what glorious exploits he went on to achieve that morning, yet deep down, we all knew he was *trying very hard to be helpful.* And later in the day, as usual, after caffeine's demon bean had finished working its wicked energy, he was found in his office (which I nicknamed "The Hammock" for reasons that may be self-evident) feet up and defenseless, snoring amidst a smattering of Sudoku puzzles.

Welcome to our world. Please wipe your feet.

Toad sat straight down in the middle of the dusty road, his legs stretched out before him, and stared fixedly in the direction of the disappearing motor-car. He breathed short, his face wore a placid satisfied expression, and at intervals he faintly murmured "Poop-poop!"... "Hi! Toad!" they cried. "Come and bear a hand, can't you!" The Toad never answered a word, or budged from his seat in the road; so they went to see what was the matter with him. They found him in a sort of a trance, a happy smile on his face, his eyes still fixed on the dusty wake of their destroyer. At intervals he was still heard to murmur "Poop-poop!"

"The Wind in the Willows," Kenneth Grahame

Chapter 2:
The Unmistakable Joys
of Driving

First, Select Your Vehicle

A car interior? Not so much. Irrespective of the many different incarnations of Tom's car over the years, each version gave the same impression: a museum of lethal artifacts that had suffered hand-grenade attack and was devoid of sufficient finances to reorganize. One always sat amidst the detritus and lowered one's feet into the foot-well nervously anticipating crackles, sparks and squelches; on high alert for animated yelps, or punctures from sources either living or inert.

On one occasion getting into Tom's car, as I clambered with due trepidation into the landfill, my eyes were drawn to pretty golden constellations twinkling beneath. Ah, live bullets. Why are there live bullets at my feet, Tom? No rational response was forthcoming, but I was apparently supposed to be sustained by the hand-waving reassurance that they were "only .22's," presumably underscoring the hypothesis that my lower limbs were somehow inoculated against invasion of such minimal diameter. I glowered disapprovingly, but otherwise retained my counsel as we pulled away.

It was then, as we turned a corner, that the bottle of radium rolled against my ankle. Radium. You're unfamiliar with the substance? That's probably a plus. The fact that radium is a heavy metal, numbered 88 in Mendeleev's table, may not spark interest; although even the partially initiated will know that a number that large can only belong to an element as unstable as an Italian government. All radium isotopes are radioactive and readily effuse radon gas. Mother Nature provides assistance by painting this biological hazard luminescent blue (Radium, not Hostetler, alas) an intrinsic warning if ever there was one.

But Tom has tired of warning labels, even Eternal ones. He is a voracious harbinger of the elements, like a power-mad monarch harvests taxes. And no pernickety bower bird is our Tom: all colors, atomic weights, physical properties and hazard levels are clutched to his fatherly bosom devoid of prejudice.

Back in the real world, SSRL's Safety Office unearthed Tom's proud trove. Intent on keeping radioactivity to a fussy minimum, safety officer Ian Evans commanded Hostetler that the radium child of his eclectic brood warranted immediate expulsion. Standing six foot three and armed with vocal reverberations of Welsh origin, Ian cuts an imposing figure when he so chooses; when forthright in his missives he is heeded by all. Even Tom obeyed; directly removing the radioactive bottle from the synchrotron building. He simply chucked it in his car instead.

Problem solved.

Hence my proximate re-acquaintance with the forbidden alpha-emitter, while in a seat I frequently occupied, reduced me to more basic emotions. My remonstrations were both loud and protracted. But Tom had driven countless miles in the self-same vehicle, and so was unfazed by what he heard as my unmanly bleating. We proceeded to lunch, while I sulked.

In fairness, I never did see the radium bottle again in Tom's car. I have no idea where it is now, although I theorize it has long since nestled within Tom's cabin in Santa Cruz, amidst the un-alphabetized glories of his residence, radiating powerfully.

No wonder his poor cat was so weird.

DIY Freeway Exits

Tom has once again folded his 6ft 1 inch frame into his tiny red Miata (a.k.a. "Little Red") and is driving home after a hard day breaking things at SSRL. The blackened mountains are crouching Chinese dragons, profiles scorched with sunset's crimson. They backdrop a weather-beaten Latino man trudging along roadside, gas can in hand. As ever, Tom wishes to help and so pulls over.

It transpires Tom and the Mexican man don't share a common language. His tongue generates only Spanish and Tom, as a typically culpable Californian resident (ditto myself), has yet to master much beyond: "Feliz Navidad!" – hardly the most functional fall-back on a year-round basis – and a limited selection of expletives. A flurry of hand-waving mime ensues and, with the empty gas can as a signature clue, intelligence is conveyed of a stranded motorist and an exhausted vehicle; the location of which is beside I-280, the Freeway languishing alongside the lab.

Tom, generous spirit in flow, motions the man into the Mazda and chauffeurs him first to the gas station to fill his can and thence to his car. But as Tom drives onto I-280's northbound on-ramp, the man signals frantically that they are heading the wrong way: the stricken vehicle lies southbound. Without pausing to think – a clause that advances strong challenge to be the title of this book – Tom flings the car off-road with a flick of the steering wheel and ploughs through the long grass of the cloverleaf interchange (Figure 2.1). For days afterwards we saw the flattened foliage testifying its wounded accusation of Tom's liberal attitude to roadway discipline.

Figure 2.1: The mad career of Little Red, with Captain Thomas E Hostetler at the helm

Allegedly, as the Miata careens off-road, the man screams approval at the resourceful solution so readily applied to their dilemma. He shouts with joy and approbation. But this is Tom's report; so whether the man really was radiating unalloyed appreciation is an interpretation I approach with considerable caution. And since he evidently wasn't shouting "Merry Christmas," his exact message has been lost to the ether. Phrases such as: "Madre de Dios! Hombre Loco!" may have actually been the centrepieces of his diction; we'll simply never know. Realistically, the idea that anyone responds with squeals of delight to being to be bounced erratically through the undergrowth between freeway lanes by a septuagenarian stranger in a toy car – for all that Tom reports it thus – prompts my innate scepticism to raise a quizzical eyebrow.

But I'm certainly prepared to believe he was screaming.

The Rear Ending that Wasn't

America permits drivers to turn right on a red light. This is a sound and helpful expansion on the highway code and I embrace the ruling wholeheartedly. (Now if only the country could figure out what a roundabout was, and how to use it, my joy would be truly unbounded. But I digress.)

However, to deliberately go *straight on* at a red light is strongly dissuaded; and with no little fuss and censure. But this prohibition forms little more than a provocative – and flimsy – challenge to our resourceful protagonist, Thomas H. You see: if a right-turn is permitted, then why not two? Turn right at the light where you wish to go straight ahead, immediately flip a U-turn, then make a second right turn and, hey presto, one has *legally* gone straight through a red light. What could possibly go wrong?

The hour once again proclaims Lunch O'clock and Tom and I are hungrily pub-ward bound. Today, Tom's driving, so we're both nestled amidst the Miata's *objects d'art*, barrelling along three inches above the asphalt. We're now at a red light and our destination: the Dutch Goose public house, is directly across from where we stand; with the Alameda de las Pulgas lying crosswise between.

There's no way she can have seen it coming.

Tom's mind stirs; which means an arthritic and addled gerbil has unwisely staggered onto the tread-wheel of his brain. Dark portents impend. Tom is strategizing – I can see it – how to dismiss the offensive red light that stands between us and the cooling libations of the lunchtime hour. Invitingly, a gas station forecourt lies immediately right, so a small reverse, foray across the gas station, left exit and then right turn will consummate sweet victory over the red light's haughty imposition.

The only tiny flaw in this perfect plan is that Tom deems it wholly unnecessary to check behind him for the presence of other vehicles before reversing. (I know, it sounds obvious now, doesn't it? Hindsight is always 20-20 and all that.) Tom simply slides the gear shift down and right, floors the gas, and slams into the gold Buick directly behind us.

I borrow the (evidently undervalued) rear-view mirror to observe the startled, bird-like face of the elderly lady into whose morning we have so rudely arrived. Mouth agog, cupping claw-like hands, she seems frozen in time, as if to ward off the demonic Miata by gesture alone. I wondered what she was thinking. Did she contemplate what she would tell her insurers? Did she fret at the prospect of convincing a worldly-wise agent that, rather than her being another older driver guilty of rear-ending a car; instead, the driver in front had been so impossibly imbecilic as to have rammed her in reverse from a standing start? She likely ruminated on her limited chances of being believed. Given that she's already 163 years old, and oblivious to all four pairs of spectacles perched atop her primly coiffured head, her credibility is slender indeed. And yet her protestations would have been entirely true. Unbeknownst, she had simply become the newest, and understandably most reluctant, member of the exclusive group of those who have a 'Tom story.'

Meanwhile, Tom merely sat beside me motionless, in his own puddle of stupidity, staring straight ahead; until I ordered him from the vehicle to make reparation. He was gone but seconds. His mission impossible was to convince the cowering crone (now scrabbling for the door-locks against the advancing maniac) that he was, in fact, entirely benign. Having concluded this enterprise in honourable – if inevitable – failure, he re-alighted the Mazda with teenage alacrity and we sped away; our scattered dust, and her shattered nerves, the only remaining testament to our adventure.

Through the Oleanders

Bethany Lyles was the only student I ever supervised. I'm grateful to her because she was as sharp as a whip and motivated to work hard, so my responsibilities decayed to almost zero. She's since gone on to study Nuclear Engineering at UC Berkeley and start a family; but for the summer of 2001 she was a vivacious cog in the happily dysfunctional family of the SSRL synchrotron staff. Attractive and a social live-wire, Bethany was a glittering participant in all our convivialities.

The pub's siren song summoned the faithful to lunch and Bethany, Dave, JR, Tom and I all dutifully heeded the call. Tom drove separately in his small, silver Ford Escort because he regularly complained that we lingered too long at lunch and, given that he was tremendously busy, he had to be back earlier. We suppressed sniggering and accommodated his independent travel knowing that on such occasions, when we arrived back at the lab, we would find him spread-eagled across a chair, dead to the world, with half-completed Sudoku puzzles splattered around his feet.

Absurdly, Tom didn't even manage to leave the pub before us. We departed simultaneously: Tom still driving solo, we four piled into my Audi. Somehow, possibly testosterone related, this had unconsciously – and highly inadvisedly – become a race. I gained early advantage from the additional seconds it took Tom to fold his arthritic skeleton into the tiny Ford and so pulled away first. The route from the Dutch Goose to SLAC affords overtaking opportunities on the dual lanes of Sand Hill Rd all the way up to the required U-turn and back again (Figure 2.2). But we had left first and, furthermore, were propelled by a 2.8 litre V6; while Tom drove the sewing-machine he'd bought for 50 bucks. By the time we reached the U-turn on Sand Hill Rd, Tom wasn't even visible in the mirror. Game over. Or so it seemed.

Figure 2.2: White arrows: the legally suggested route from the Dutch Goose to SLAC. Circled black arrow: Tom's more creative itinerary

As we cruised down the home straight, the tall oleander bushes in the central divide rustled urgently, and then suddenly, simply exploded. From a blast of leaves and petals a small silver car was jettisoned; careening wildly across the road in front of us with a grinning white-haired madman at the wheel. Tom had simply slammed the little vehicle up onto the central divide, through the vegetation and onto the East-bound carriageway, trusting his then-59-year-old reflexes to cope with whatever he landed near (or on) on the other side of the bushes. Dave and Bethany respectively roared and squealed in delight; JR's mouth fell open and made noises that weren't quite words. We picked oleander leaves off his car for days.

Of course if any of us had tried this manoeuver we would have hit a car, or encountered a cop, or both; and been instantly hauled downtown to be grilled with questions we had no chance of satisfactorily answering. But Tom, with the luck – and evident blessing – of the Devil himself, miraculously encountered free road-space and hadn't even grounded out on the central divide.

And he won the race. Dammit.

Pinball Parking

Parking at SSRL is a chess game pitting creative chutzpah against authority. On one side, the security guards must maintain safe order; on the other, staff want to park within an hour's walk of their workplace. No-one is guilt-free. Security sometimes mindlessly forbids even *safe* parking if there's no painted lines; and staff creativity can verge upon the blatantly disobedient. I myself have to confess complicity in the Case of the Missing 'No Parking' Sign that we used to irritatingly discover in the most park-able of unmarked spaces. (They'll find Jimmy Hoffa first.)

Yet one man stood out in infamy. Tom's cars would be most egregiously placed: in government spots, cordoned-off zones and even on sidewalks; triggering an over-reaction from some security who hounded him mercilessly forever after.

Figure 2.3: Blocking a sidewalk and on a red kerb. Problem, officer?

But Tom also employed a "pinball parking" strategy that compromised his high favour even among SSRL staff, since several were car fanatics. His most common target, fortunately, was merely the hillside, which he frequently employed as a landing pad. Each morning his front license plate was squashed into a new shape against the hill (see: "How to Park a Car"). But other vehicles could also find employment as buffers to his parking protocol; and no object was truly off limits as Ricochet Ronnie (a.k.a. Tom) clattered his way around our parking lot.

Departing for home one day in 2013, Tom finally committed a truly capital offense. He hit the jackpot – quite literally hit – of parking-lot crime: he bumped JR's pristine, ivory-coloured hulk of a GMC Denali. And did so right in front of its owner.

JR is pathologically protective of his prized vehicles; he shields them as if constructed entirely from rice-paper. To door-ding his car is a sin of Biblical proportions; if he merely contemplates a dent, this can trigger convulsions. He occasionally parks on a gravel strip nearly a mile from the synchrotron to avoid a scratch; and while this is successful in preserving bodywork, it somewhat undermines the purpose of having a car at all. Should JR's beloved chariot suffer impact, even if no harder than the kiss of an unaffectionate mosquito, he is catapulted into paroxysms of emotion. So when he witnessed Tom brainlessly bouncing his Toyota Celica off the treasured Denali's fender simply to avoid having to look behind him, JR was not soothed by a tantric mood of inner peace. Rather, he roared threats of bodily retribution at ear-buggering volume.

Brilliantly, in an iconic example of The Wake, a security officer happened to be walking by and JR was immediately accosted by the long arm of the law. Painfully over-zealous, the officer recorded all JR's ill-chosen imprecations of death and dismemberment in her Notebook of Shame and JR, metaphorically at least, was hauled away for judgment. Days later it took him several rounds of patiently reciting teary-eyed remorse and heartfelt penitence to roomfuls of dour HR overlords in order to paddle out of The Wake's newest riptide.

Tom, on the other hand, despite having caused the collision, was left as free as a bird. He simply drew another hearty lungful of tobacco from his trusty corncob and zoomed homewards; most likely careening off several other vehicles on his way out of the parking lot.

Beep beep!

Tom Fought the Law and the – Law Won

2012 was a time of economic hardship. Congressional and Senate Houses were displaying above-average levels of selfish incompetence and everyone was feeling the pinch. An automatic vehicle gate was installed at the Alpine Road entrance to SLAC, to save money by replacing the security station there. The two iron-barred doors are fifteen feet high and open concertina fashion, triggered by proximity sensor of a valid SLAC badge. One vehicle only should enter per green light; a second vehicle quickly 'piggybacking' through is *strictly* forbidden.

Immediately, and insanely, Tom decided a feasibility study was in order to see if a second vehicle could indeed get through before the massive gates closed and pincered it like an accordion. His vehicle, to be precise. Good plan, Tom.

Now the piggybacking prohibition was vehement; not just because of the risk of human injury and mechanical damage if there's a collision between gate and car, but also because three years earlier a former employee, who sadly was mentally unwell, had piggybacked onto the premises through a pedestrian gate and committed sabotage to the tune of $500 000. This back-story might dissuade mere mortals like you and me from trialling our very own (pointless) experiment. Not so our fearless hero, Thomas H! He saw this legal threat as a worthy windmill at which to tilt. And the icing of intelligence on this cake of sound thinking was that Tom piggybacked through the gate even *before* the human guards had been removed.[1] Brilliant!

Thus the security officers were still standing there, that cold January morning, scarcely believing their eyes, as they spied the familiar miscreant Miata whizz through the gate, piggybacking directly under their noses; and then sputter away up the

---

[1] View Tom's escapade for yourself: http://youtu.be/9_ZAhdVSgU4

frosted hill at the non-breakneck escape speed of 25 mph, on the three cylinders that still fired. They had ample time to exchange commiserating eye-rolls, finish their coffee and warm their hands before boarding their vehicle to lasso the inept criminal.

On capture, Tom carefully explained, with the patience of a long-suffering father, how his actions were an invaluable test of perimeter security and how the officers should therefore be grateful to him for his demonstration. Astonishingly (at least to Tom) this iron-clad defence did not prevail. His explanations were, in fact, less than favourably received and his name wended its weary way onto a Naughty Ticket once again.

Other SLAC security stories just tell themselves:

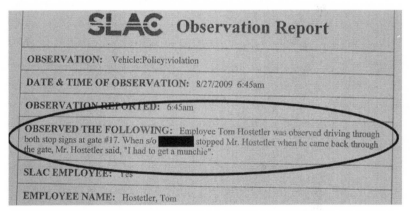

Figure 2.4: But of course

Nor is it only uniformed officers issuing Tom reprimand. Tom receives civilian citations too; stern advisories from Joe Public. The newest, from the latest citizen left floundering in The Wake, simply read:

"WATCH WHERE YOU'RE GOING NEXT TIME, A******!!"

Of course Tom, bless him, was innocently clueless as to either the time or nature of his infraction and merely handed round the note to us at work in a state of wounded surprise.

Learning to Fly

Over the years Tom has confessed a host of motorized mishaps. And given that he is seldom fazed enough to remember such incidents, and his memory is not the best anyway, one can only speculate what catalogue of catastrophe the historical picture truly holds.

Many of Tom's vehicular misadventures did not even involve any other party: Tom was skilled enough to crash solo. He would simply slip out of resonance with his immediate surroundings, and be disappointed to find Mother Nature callously inflexible in yielding to his perception of where the road now might be. This difference of opinion triggered the time Tom flew off the mountainside of Highway 9, to provide some impromptu restructuring, many meters beneath, to a citizen's retaining wall. It also accounts for the time Tom was mildly surprised to discover himself suspended upside-down in a tree aside Los Trancos Road, after an overly exuberant ride down the hill, with his mangled motorbike steaming and spluttering beneath. (No doubt Tom's guardian angel has applied for a transfer several dozen times and is currently on the astral version of Prozac. But this is a theological digression we may not need.)

In the former case, 'Little Red' the Miata landed at the bottom of the hill after its brief maiden flight, planted in an understandably flustered woman's garden wall. Christian she may be, but I doubt this was the visitation from the skies for which she prayed. Tom phoned for a tow-truck, to haul the surprisingly little-damaged car back topside; indicating his position on Highway 9 via a distinctive temporary road sign above.

He then immediately rethought: Since there's a crash, authorities may be notified; and even his small amount of dinner wine may imply him falsely guilty of more than mere inattention

– especially as he had spilled some all over himself, as per usual. In a rare moment of caution, he adjudged it necessary to expunge every alcohol molecule absorbed before receiving assistance. But this would require more time than was likely available before the tow-truck arrived. What to do?

Unusually panicked, Tom scrambled up the hill, wrestled the roadsign he had given as a beacon of his position from its seating and flung it down-slope into the leaf litter, very effectively sabotaging the rescue he had just requested. This presaged a strenuous regimen of sprints, jumps and push-ups to metabolize the booze. Of course the poor tow-truck driver is now searching for a road sign he no longer has any realistic chance of finding as he meanders back and forth in the mountains. Welcome to The Wake, friend. That said, if he should spot a white-haired man in evening dress by the roadside who has suddenly turned Zumba Ninja, he could take that as a reasonable clue.

I wonder what you would have witnessed that autumn evening, were you a passing cyclist. The last glimmers of daylight permeate the multi-coloured mosaic of leaves as you glide gracefully down the road's scenic curves. Perhaps Keats' poetry charms your attention: "Season of mists and mellow fruitfulness," or some similar reflection. Or maybe you just absorb the tranquil scene with free-wheeling mind, as staccato bird chatter punctures the earthy aroma exhaling upwards and the evening rolls lazily forward. And then suddenly, pelting round the corner towards you charges a pensioner in a cowboy hat and wine-stained tuxedo, wild-eyed and panting, with bony knees pistoning everywhere as if training for the Marines.

It's enough to change the mood a fraction, I should think.

Collaborative Driving

Not all Tom's driving anecdotes are as dramatic as flying off mountainsides, slapping oncoming cars (see: "Party Like it's 1999") or adopting inverted crucifixion postures in roadside trees. Yet nor do they need to be to qualify for the distinctive hallmark of the 'Tom story.'

Early 1998: I'd been in America a month. We were hurtling along Foothill expressway in Tom's red pickup on a lunchtime foray when he suddenly wanted to light his pipe. Without warning, Tom simply took both hands from the wheel to pack his cob from a tobacco pouch that had materialized from nowhere. The road had a high camber so the truck quickly started veering right. Within a two-count we'd left the roadway and, seeing that Tom was absorbed wholly in his nicotine need, his eyebrows knitted in concentration and his fingers spooning scented tobacco into the pipe bowl, while our future lay ditch-wards, I grabbed the wheel and steered us back into lane.

"I thought you'd figure it out," Tom mumbled indistinctly, his clamped jaws now occupied in guiding pipe to flame. I was still steering from the passenger's side a minute later – Tom grumbling about the tobacco's dampness – when we were again in difficulty: this time closing rapidly on a sedan at twelve o'clock. It wasn't clear how I could help this time.

"Tom, you're still in charge of the speed!"

"Oh, that's right," he remembered, slamming on the anchors to avoid imminent collision, "I was wondering what you were playing at for a minute."

Another time I was returning a rental car. My Audi's rear fender had been repaired from its latest playdate with yet another

US citizen congenitally bewildered about the concept of braking in stop-and-go traffic, and Tom, as ever, helped out. Upon receipt of my mended motor, Tom stuck out his hand for its keys. "Oh hell no," I thought (and possibly said aloud). But what choice did I have? We still had two cars and I alone was insured to drive the rental. I was compelled to surrender my newly-repaired-and-gleaming A6 to Tom's control. It was only three miles back to the rental office, I reassured myself, unconvincingly. I took off, Tom following.

Like Lot's wife, I couldn't resist looking back, even though I knew I'd probably be punished even worse than her. Glancing in the rear-view mirror with a well-justified sense of doom, I saw only a blur of thrashing limbs. Tom had morphed into a demented octopus: hell-bent on simultaneously altering every setting. I saw him frantically slapping and yanking-at every button, knob and lever he could reach; with all the grace and fluency of a man being attacked by killer bees. And while it's true there was a low afternoon sun, the sun-visors – both of them – were being flapped up and down spastically, as if his life depended on him signaling the entirety of "War and Peace" in Morse Code before we arrived.

We reached the rental office and I hurried over to my car to triage the effects of Tom's brief stewardship. "Here," he said as he clambered out, "I broke this," and poured a few shards of fractured plastic into my hand, later determined to be the remains of the driver's sun-visor clip. He sounded somehow disappointed he hadn't achieved more. I was just surprised he wasn't out of breath.

"Watch This!"

Tom Hostetler

Chapter 3:
Tom's Invaluable Guide:
"How To"

How to Take a Nap

We've all been there. Those turgid afternoons when the eyelids, as if by alchemy, turn to lead and the head begins the inescapable jerks that precursor the unplanned nap. I have myself suffered the ignominiously dimpled cheeks of 'keyboard-face' from the unintentional post-lunch snooze.

But one man stands alone as champion. Tom. Not only does he possess the ability to re-energize himself on the slenderest of shut-eyes; he also has the *laissez-faire* to bed down simply *anywhere*. In years gone by, Tom would even position his truck in a central lane of I-280 southbound and nod off; his alarm-clock the vibration of the truck running over the raised bumps delineating the lanes. Tom assures me that he hasn't done that since the low traffic levels of the 70's. I feigned reassurance, but my horrified expression was frozen in place for several days.

Once we were in a group meeting when I saw Tom perform the signature shoulder-nestling against his chair, as a cat kneads his bed-to-be, before tilting the Hat over his face to bid conscious goodbye to the world, directly across the table from his dumbfounded boss, who had called the meeting. Moreover, Bart, said manager, had specifically asked the on-call operators to take station at a prominent bridge, as visible comfort to the working lab. But it's arguable how comforting it was on the occasions when the entire slew of scientists merely witnessed that our ship's captain, when Tom, had once more vacated to the Happy Land of Nod. The temptation to creep up and shout: "ICEBERG AHOY!" in his ear, to see him spring upwards with limbs flailing, loomed large at such times, but I never actually did.

Sometimes Tom's collapses into coma were less than accidental. He would be found feet up, cozily bundled in a lab coat, underneath a blanket, wearing noise-canceling head-phones

(Figure 3.1). Far from 'nodding off,' it was clear he had entered the realms of 'aiding and abetting willful slumber.' And if he were the on-call beamline operator then, ever ingenious, he would set the cellphone to vibrate mode and strap it to his skull using the earphones' headband.

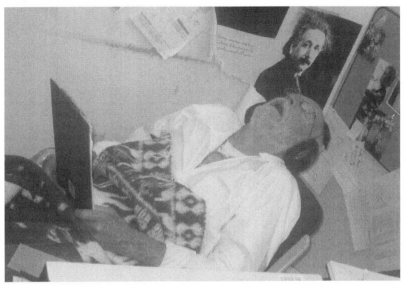

Figure 3.1: Your tax dollars at work: Captain Nite-Nite goes hard at it at SSRL (2011), Sudoku puzzle in hand. In the background Einstein looks on, understandably unimpressed

These creature comforts could greatly extend Tom's time in the subterranean realm of repose. The end of his shift would sail past with an unheard *whoosh* while he lay back in his chair, mouth wide enough to swallow the sky. When I was still a research scientist, many was the time I was working late and espied Tom emerge from his reveries well into the evening. He would regard his rediscovered universe with foggy uncertainty, blink owlishly, and toddle off into the evening's faintly luminous gloom. I would joke that, in credit to his integrity, at least he never charged overtime for the hours he slept past quitting time. And in credit to his wits, he eventually learned to slip past me from a side-door on such occasions, to escape my merciless hoots of derision at his tardy resurrection.

How to Park a Car

Part 1: At Work (2012)

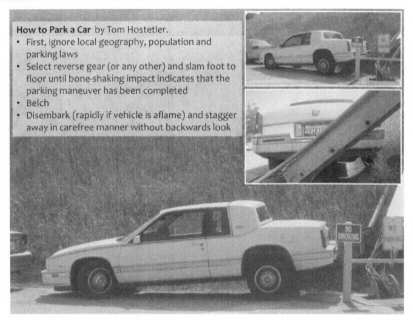

How to Park a Car by Tom Hostetler.
* First, ignore local geography, population and parking laws
* Select reverse gear (or any other) and slam foot to floor until bone-shaking impact indicates that the parking maneuver has been completed
* Belch
* Disembark (rapidly if vehicle is aflame) and stagger away in carefree manner without backwards look

Figure 3.2: Tom demonstrates his parking strategy with his 1988 Cadillac

Part 2: At Home (2014)

For those of us who own glasses, we know they can be a nuisance. And never more so than when we're separated from them, because then one is caught in the double-jeopardy predicament of searching for something which is 98% invisible precisely while one's eyesight is compromised. I have myself been reduced to the pathetic, squinting figure on hands and knees, padding around my wooden floors imploring the heavens to help find the wretched things. We've all lost them. Dropped them. The less competent of us have even sat on them. But have you ever driven over your own glasses while parking your car?

You see even here Tom is in a different class. I was with him when he discovered this achievement.

Perchance you wish to join this elite group, please give your best attention to Tom's "How To" recipe for frame-squishing, lens-crunching goodness:

- Day 1: Arrive home; park in usual space. Alight from vehicle with the delicacy of being ejected from a military jet, scattering possessions over a generous radius as if by grenade. Blithely wander off into the darkness with little to no sense of what may be missing. Try not to be fazed by the fact that your house and all contents therein are now mysteriously out of focus.

- Day 2: Awaken just enough sodden gray cells to deduce your glasses are missing. Conduct fruitless search of domicile, obtain spare pair and proceed to work. Later, return and drive over first pair with sniper-like precision while parking, all the while being as oblivious to your actions as a Kardashian to culture and social graces.

Figure 3.3: Nope, they're done for

- Day 3: Discover the fruits of your genius. Expend a few sad minutes chattering senselessly about how you can fix them, even though the frames are pancake flat and both lenses are crushed to fine powder. Haplessly wiggle the frame as if any of what you've said makes sense (Figure 3.3) before allowing a helpful friend[1] to persuade you that your application of a 2 000 lb Toyota rolling pin has, in fact, rendered them total goners.

As Dave was to later comment: "That's our boy!"

---

[1] Admittedly the definition of 'helpful' may be compromised by said friend being doubled over with thigh-slapping guffaws and taking pictures.

How to Fly a Forklift

Figure 3.4: The airborne Allis-Chalmers ACC 30 LP forklift plane in building IR12, as rigged by Tom. (One also can't help noticing the bottle of beer, circled, in the right-hand foreground)

As ever, a picture speaks a thousand words. Tom once seated himself in a 5 000 lb forklift rigged to a 30 ton crane (Figure 3.4). The crane hook travels along an I-beam drivable between two other, orthogonal, I-beams fixed at either end of the building, which traverse the roof length. As a result the crane hook can hover above any point of the building floor. Of critical relevance, Tom has the crane's remote control box in his lap.

Thus, we arrive at the disturbing conclusion that Tom can now fly himself around the building. In his forklift.

This event predates my arrival at SSRL, so I was not direct witness to the lunatic in the levitating leviathan propelling two steel prongs of death around IR12 at disemboweling height. Yet in fairness to Tom, OSHA specifies no limit on the safe altitude or airspeed of a forklift, so he is technically OSHA-compliant.

IR12 is also the building in which the magnets which constrain SSRL's orbiting electrons were fabricated. The magnet cores are laminated steel and copper windings are fixed around them. The steel laminates are glued together and the reaction is exothermic: i.e. the glue gets hot as it cures. One has to wait for the magnet to cool before the next assembly stage can proceed.

Re-enter The Hat, with all his inherent ingenuity, to speed the cooling process. Or was it just another excuse to play with the crane? Either way, it was from there Tom suspended each hot magnet in the center of the building and, using a guide rope, hauled the 500 lb mass towards one wall. And let go.

You get the principle: it's to air-cool the magnet. But the result is a red-hot pendulum, the weight of a car's engine block, oscillating the room six feet over everyone's heads. The building manager, a man whose sins were hardly of requisite magnitude to deserve having to supervise Hostetler, nixed the process at first glance. For one thing, it wasn't effectively cooling the magnet and for another, someone was obviously going to die.

Undaunted, Tom dumped the magnet into the back of SSRL's F150 truck. His newest theory was to drive up and down I-280 as fast as possible, cooling the magnet as it slid about unrestrained in the pickup bed, threatening to break through the tailgate and crush the nearest Prius. This too was a bust. In the end, the time-honored practice of patience was the only solution.

But not for lack of Tom trying very hard to be helpful.

How to Shake a Paint Can

For many years SSRL's machine shop was overseen by two very genial machinists: Nels and Frank. I have no picture of Frank, but if you visualize an older version of Super Mario, that's pretty much perfect. Not only that, but Frank was as cheery and bouncy as his computer-game doppelganger too; we never saw him annoyed.

Except once. Good job, Tom.

Tom had a painting task to do (ironically, the very one that earned the Environmental Stewardship Award pictured earlier). As often, the paint can needed to be shaken first, but Tom was not going to waste his own effort to shake paint and, creativity ever to the fore, knew precisely what to do.

Figure 3.5: SSRL paint shaker, occasionally misused for machining parts

That's how it was found. The SSRL machine shop lathe (Figure 3.5, sans paint can) was rolling over and over at slow speed with a paint can loaded in its jaws – eccentrically, to maximize internal agitation – yet, worst of all, without a man in sight. Poor Frank. It was his job to ensure safe operation of the workshop machines, yet here was one running unmanned. The supervision requirement was understandably rigid given the tragic April 2011 death of a university student using a lathe at Yale. In fairness to Tom, it seems unlikely that any truly unsafe scenario could have unfolded, although it teases the mind to envisage that one could have later discovered an empty can rotating methodically, having vomited its contents across the shop, with potentially beautiful linear splatters of yellow up the walls and across the ceilings and floors: our machine shop's very own Jackson Pollock.

Meanwhile, Detective Frank was on the case. On the one hand no fingerprints were lifted, so theoretically the violator could never be known. Yet on the other hand he needed two fewer than three guesses to know exactly who was to blame.

Frank was angry, for the first time in our history. The corridors of SSRL, usually reserved for the signature whistles and call-signs between staff, reverberated to the rare tone of displeasure. Frank's Latino passion was aflame, and Tom's insouciance only fuelled the fire. For Tom's part, he later took a curious, if unintentional, revenge against the administrator of this seemingly harsh justice: he completely forgot who Frank was. To this day Tom remains unable to recall his face, despite them having worked in the same building for over a decade.

We ribbed Tom mercilessly about the incident, and his memory. Yet one should not think of Tom as a victim here, or possibly ever. A few years later, in 2014, I needed to upgrade my machine shop skills with some lathe proficiency and approached Tom for training. He simply looked me up and down and said:

"How can I? You don't even have a paint can."

Touché.

Once Upon a Tom

How to Give and Take Advice

<u>Giving Advice: Part 1 (2003)</u>
"If anybody comes, just run."

It's hard to think how that could ever form a sane suggestion. The actual context involved a summer intern and the SSRL crane (Figure 3.6). Steel hutch wall panels, rigged via suction cups, needed to be lifted upstairs, but the intern did not possess the requisite training to operate the 1 000 lb crane. Hence Tom's advice, the centrepiece of his highly dubious authorization.

One can only imagine the scene, were a safety officer to stroll on deck

Figure 3.6: SSRL crane

and find a 170 lb steel plate twelve feet airborne, swinging lightly in the breeze, with no evidence of humanity except the fading sound of sprinting footsteps. But again, Tom's luck held.

<u>Receiving Advice: Part 1</u>

Tom's wife Joanna was leaving town for several weeks. She'd hidden her car keys, advising Tom that she didn't want him driving her Saturn, for fear he would crash it. Tom was insulted at the impugning of his abilities, so hunted down the keys and drove the car anyway, to keep the engine ticking over.

He crashed it, of course. He'd pulled over to scavenge some sunglasses discarded by the side of the road and, reversing back to collect the two-dollar treasures, slammed into a guard rail he didn't see. The rear fender was mangled beyond repair. Thus began a mad scramble to complete the replacement before spousal return, which was successfully, if shamefacedly, achieved.

Giving Advice: Part 2 (2009)

Tom was working with a female colleague to determine the native molecular state of arsenic, using broad spectrum x-ray illumination on BL2-2. In the context of groping for answers Tom emailed her the solicitation: "Please indulge my groping."

Fortunately the colleague was well aware of Tom's daft applications of the English language and no damage was done; nor was Tom forced into sensitivity classes for the next decade.

Receiving Advice: Part 2 (2001)

Tom was driving to lunch with Bart. Their destination was the Stanford golf course cafeteria, lying at two-o'clock to their direction of travel. Bart indicated the construction site (later the Hewlett and Flora Family Foundation buildings) that was directly in line with their destination; especially noting the 15 foot high pile of construction dirt.

"Bet you wouldn't drive up that earth mound!" challenged Bart, uncharacteristically foolishly. (What was Bart thinking?! By now you will have mouthed a solemn vow never to share a ride, or even roadway, with Hostetler; and will have a good feel for the wisdom of *goading* Tom into vehicular folly.)

No second inducement was required. The light turned green, Tom flung the car off-road and, not five seconds later, the tiny silver Ford sat proudly atop the huge pile of dirt.

No construction workers were present, nor did the car sink irretrievably into the mud; again purely through Hostetler's unbreakable good fortune. One can only speculate what open-mouthed expressions of disbelief and displeasure would be seen beneath the hard-hats as construction workers stared at the zany, grinning pilot of the madcap car on the mud-heap; and the penitent passenger white-knuckling the dashboard, reciting long-forgotten Hail Marys in continuous loop.

How to Write a Shift Report

Tom is occasionally overcome with an overwhelming desire for accuracy. When recording the day's events in a shift report, as the beamline operator is required to do, Tom often insists events are recorded at the exact minute they occurred.

17:03	Dayshift, Saturday,	T_Hostetler	Log: 19-Apr-14
		SSRL-BLDO	715414

```
09:22  BL11-3 Detector continuously reporting busy.
09:43  Session restart fixed the problem.

09:45  Checked in with 13-1.  Stefano reported that
       they've not had the  polarization they
       expected since the 20:16 dump-and-fill last night.
       Waiting for Ohldag to come to the lab.

10:26  BL13-1 asks for a dump-and-fill with new parameters
       Worked out between BL13-1 and SPEAR Operator.

10:55  Polled the users and chose 11:10 for dump-and-fill time.

11:10  Dumped the beam to alter the lattice.

11:28  SPEAR Oper stopped the injection at 55mA to measure the
       effect of the lattice change at BL13-1.  BLs 4,7,&11 opene
       to make use of the 55 mA.
```

Figure 3.7: A Military-style Hostetler shift report (2014)

When queried, Tom attributes this predilection for precision to his military background: three years aboard the nuclear submarine USS Andrew Jackson. At such times Tom sternly exhorts his work colleagues to comparable strictness, too. He has hounded the systems manager, synchrotron operators and anyone who will listen to synchronize every report system on site to the second. But what Tom seems charmingly unaware of is that his fugues of military meticulousness are but a passing fancy. At any moment they can be replaced with his more common *modus operandi*: a hippy-chick style insouciance bordering on abandon (Figure 3.8). You'll notice in this second shift report that there are no time stamps at all, not even for the outlandishly spurious report of the unfortunate animal. At the time it triggered the immediate response shown beneath: please excuse the more energized language which generates in the moment.

```
04:59   Dayshift Wednesday, 2013-11-13                          Log: 14-Nov-13
                                                                      687903

        Dayshift Wednesday, 2013-11-13

        Progman: Bart Johnson

        Mode: 500 mA, frequent fill

        BL-13 closed

        Injured deer in the east driveway;  650-363-4953.

        No complaints.

        No faults.
```

For hell's sake, Hostetler, what kind of drug-induced shift report is this?

a) We don't really need a wildlife report, you loony
b) Are you trying to imply the deer has a frigging cellphone?
c) By: "No faults" are you perhaps overlooking the *seven* faults recorded during your shift, including three oxygen deficiency alerts, the crashing of Beamline 9 and the faulted Liquid Nitrogen system, where the main valve closed and all LN monos were temporarily cut off from their essential cooling supply? That sort of "No faults" you mean?
d) Your shift report is, in fact, 12 hours late. Guess you were a little too eager scampering out the door to get drunk to send it last night

Eeeesssh.

Figure 3.8: A hippy-style Hostetler shift report (2013) – and response

I'm fascinated to imagine Tom's inner reasoning. Notify operations staff of the main LN valve closure? No need. Send a tear-jerking lament of how we couldn't save Bambi? Essential! One 2014 shift report literally listed the color of all 24 lights (green or red) on a display panel – the detail was baffling. And yet we knew the next report could easily have been: "A tree fell over. I felt sad." Such are Hostetler's fluctuations of style. One day he's badgering some poor colleague towards an eye-watering level of exactness; the very next he strolls across the parking lot, with pipe-smoke still coiling from his corncob, and sticks his head directly into the flammable liquids cabinet to look for something.

"Working with Tom is a box of chocolates," grumbles a voice from the grave, "never know what you're going to get."

I hear you, Bill. But we wouldn't have it any other way.

How to Catch a Spider

SSRL is populated by black widow spiders. But our resplendence of novel resources place us well-equipped to fight back. When a security guard called me to dispatch a large black widow by Beamline 4, I overcame the arachnid by sluicing a veritable tsunami of liquid nitrogen into her web. Game over.

But Tom never killed spiders: rather, he captured them. Yet capture is contrary to their aims, so resourcefulness is required. Enter Hostetler's spider catcher (Figure 3.9). The tube is long enough to catch your spider from a standing position. Place the flexible, poly-vinyl acrylate tube-end over the spider of choice. Suck. Ideally, your target is drawn upwards to the shield a few inches from the mouth of yourself, the captor, and you can transfer the tube end into a bottle to release the spider. What could possibly go wrong?

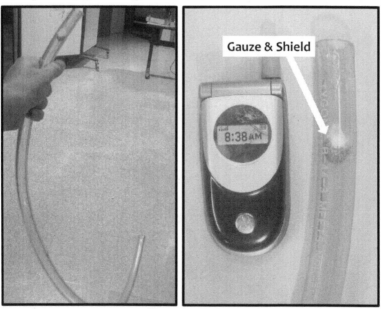

Figure 3.9: The Spider-Sucker in its entirety (left) and up close to show the copper shield & gauze designed to stop the captor swallowing the spider (right). The cell-phone is shown for scale

Yet on early application of this amazing device, things did go wrong. Tom inhaled *too hard* and the black widow, apparently more delicately assembled by our Creator to be ready for Hostetler (aren't we all) whizzed up the tube at a speed which, while likely to satisfy all her adrenalin-junkie needs, left her anatomically unprepared for impact against the copper shield. She dissembled into constituent parts on contact and Tom reported getting "some goo" in his mouth. Since he did not die from asphyxiation of a massively swollen throat and tongue, evidently said goo was not the powerful neurotoxin for which the species is infamous. He learned to suck more gently thereafter.

For all Tom's craziness risks life, limb and sanity (both ours and his) there are times where we gain vital knowledge from his inane escapades. Despite all the gray hairs we get, it would be ungentlemanly not to applaud the invaluable tuition we receive at his hand. I learned a great deal about black widows precisely because Tom confined them in bottles, rather than rendering them two-dimensional beneath a boot, as the rest of us did.

The females are astonishingly beautiful: ebony black with violin-shaped belly-marks cast in murderous scarlet. Males are scruffy brown with the same violin-mark in tired yellow. Invariably on combat the female defeats the male. She lays her jaws on one of the male's many knees, which provide access to the soft interior, and bites down again and again. Finally, before death, the male spews clear poison from his mouth: whether his or hers I never learned. Equally interestingly, when a large, glossy female is pitched against a pale, ill-fed one, it's the skinny girl, hell-bent on feeding, who wins. If you're used to catch-weight boxing bets you need to re-learn fast: in the black widow's world Bantam beats Heavy every time. We were all at Stanford, but only the schoolhouse of Hostetler gave this course.

How to Catch a Lion

One of the joys of California is the wildlife one observes. In nearly twenty years I've seen everything from sky-borne golden eagles and pelicans; to landlocked coyotes and jack-rabbits; to the marine riches of dolphins and gray whales.

And a single mountain lion in 2009. Herein lies the story.

Chris and Jen were visiting from Ontario. I toured them around SLAC, casually mentioning that despite never having seen one, mountain lions regularly stalked the site (for deer). "Like that one over there?" asked Jen innocently from the back seat. I glanced behind. She prowled with signature feline grace: rolling muscular shoulders proudly atop a lowered, focused head (the lion, not Jen). With superb irony, she was alongside Building 666. I had anticipated a super-sized domestic cat, but she was bigger: half the size of an African lioness. We stopped and scrambled out. She entered the ravine between us yet, despite my bright orange T-shirt, didn't see us. As she closed, I signaled our presence, scuffing my feet. The cat looked directly up at us (Figure 3.10, inset 2) and, with evident calculation, slinked off into the adjacent bush, secreted from our view.

"If Tom were here I bet he'd march down this ravine for a closer look," I babbled. Chris and Jen both smiled, presumably in polite disbelief. We sped off to fetch the others from the synchrotron floor. We returned with Dave and Tom aboard to the ravine edge where she had entered. I indicated the bush; was she still there? And, true to prophecy, no sooner had the vehicle halted than Tom bailed out and strode forthrightly down the ravine, despite hissed warnings and threats from Dave and me.

Tom initially circled around the bush (Figure 3.10). Then he advanced directly upon it, whereupon I had to pocket my camera and pick up rocks to hurl at the lion should it attack. Tom's preservation, regrettably, had to take precedence over the superbly marketable photographs of his deserved laceration and engorgement. I had at least secretly determined that one rock would be reserved to tag him. After all, it wasn't the poor lion's fault she was being mercilessly pursued by a nut.

Figure 3.10: Lion. Tom. Stupidity. Enough said

Tom arrived at the bush's edge and gave the outer tendrils an experimental waggle. Good job, Tom. What his back-up plan was, were he to be met with a maelstrom of claws and fangs, is unclear. Placate the monster with soothing quotes from the Dalai Lama? I truly don't know. We held our breath. And then we saw the lion silently pad away from Tom, from the smaller bush to the larger bush on the left. Dave got to see her too: at least her proud hindquarters and thick tail. But Tom couldn't see anything from the other side of the bush.

Tom alone has never seen a mountain lion. The universe holds an insuperable justice; and often it is dispensed quietly.

"Ho! Ho! Ho! To the bottle I go
To heal my heart and drown my woe
Rain may fall, and wind may blow
And many miles be still to go
But under a tall tree will I lie
And let the clouds go sailing by."
"The Fellowship of the Ring," J.R.R. Tolkien

Chapter 4:
Party On, Wayne

Hurricane House Guest

He started by breaking a glass. This was just a warm-up.

Tom is a gregarious creature: his kindness, sharp wit and easy grace rightly render him a social favorite. But the hosting environment usually retains permanent scars: one tracks Tom's social path as one tracks a tornado. His long limbs are energized by discourse yet remain unaware of local geography; at such times he is a man constructed entirely of elbows. Whirring elbows. Don Quixote may have tilted against windmills, but he wouldn't have stood a chance against Hostetler. Not only would the heroic hidalgo have been instantly unhorsed, he would also be surprised to discover that his lance was now on fire. And Tom wouldn't have even known he was there.

So just breaking a glass he had incongruously decided to twirl in my kitchen was mere *hors d'oeuvres*. Crockery, houseplants and electronics have all been sent spiraling to their functional doom by the ill-constrained limbs and pratfalls of my co-worker.

His highest ranking scalp to date is an SSRL laptop I was stewarding. It never really stood a chance. It was on, while Tom and I sipped wine in my living room. With a single swipe of his errant left paw, while illustrating some deep philosophical point only the truly illuminated (or perhaps truly inebriated) could hope to appreciate, he smacked a glass of Sauvignon Blanc (*my* glass, naturally; heaven forbid he should spill his own) onto the keyboard. With a sharp spit and blue flash the laptop instantly darkened forever. In fairness, he actually felt bad about that one.

Another time, as Tom staggered back into my house from a quick draw on his corn-cob pipe, I heard the sound of floral shredding and my floorboards sounding the hearty thump of Nature's 'Man Down' alarm. Hostetler had gone base-over-apex behind the couch; obliterating a six-foot banana palm on his way down. A muffled slur of "Sorry!" arose from the debris, like an entirely inadequate phoenix.

Tom has since been informed that he is strictly an outdoor pet. He is welcome to scamper around my yard in his charmingly haphazard style (though even this is likely to cost me a fence-panel or two) but voyages into the interior are by escort only, observing all posted signs and warnings.

An iconic memory is a night in 2003 we dedicated to a poker duel – dealer's choice – setting a bank of $50 each. If we went out on the town we could easily have spent more; so it was relatively inexpensive fun. I wrestled with one thing: I believe one is only safe from gambling's characteristic psychological damage *if* the winnings are sufficiently small that one doesn't truly desire them. $50 was close to that boundary then, I was poor, so I mused on returning Tom's money if I won it.

I need never have worried.

Tom is quite the demon at Texas Hold'em and the night paid out much of her spool to oversee our combat. Yet finally my staid perseverance at 5-card straight secured victory and I stood $50 to the good. As the horizon threatened to rebirth the sun anew, Tom scythed his right arm (he is left-handed by nature, but ambidextrous in destruction) into an open bottle of full-bodied Australian Shiraz; which belly-flopped onto my virginally white sheepskin rug and duly disgorged its dark red bounty. Hours after the bellowing had subsided (mine of recrimination, Tom's of self-justification); the drycleaner applied consummate skill to remove the stain from my rug and outright banditry to remove a staggering $49.40 from my wallet.

I pocketed the remaining 60 cents of the winnings with a conscience whiter than a drycleaner's dream.

Explosive Patio Guest

Mistress Lunchtime occasionally opened her arms wide enough to embrace a full afternoon affair. One such summery day in 2000, JR ushered us to his Menlo Park property in full mother-hen mode; not only because he is generous enough to invite us all, but also because he is prohibitively nervous about drinking beer more than half a mile from his residence, perchance he will never make it home. His paranoia is legendary.

That's how we find ourselves: Dave, Tom and I, standing in JR's long driveway by pool and patio (necessarily outdoors, since the requirements to enter his domicile are significantly more stringent than for an undocumented Arab to enter the US) basking resplendent in California's afternoon luxury. JR himself had yet to arrive; we awaited him supping afternoon ales.

That's when Tom decided to explode bullets. As you do.

Bullets were easily on hand, being scattered liberally throughout Tom's vehicle. You may know it doesn't require a gun to detonate a bullet; one merely needs to strike the shell's rear window where the firing pin connects and the bullet will go off: many have achieved this using a hammer and nail. Invariably they gain a wonderful instruction in Newton's third law too, since without the gun the bullet behaves differently. The lead slug is now the heavier component; the brass casing the lighter. As the gunpowder explodes, the bullet ambles forward lazily but the shell takes off at high speed backwards, usually engaging the person who just detonated it. There's a telltale scar you'll see on the hands of those who've learned their physics this way.

But Tom had a more grandiose idea in mind. He had with him a powerful catapult (I have no idea why) and theorized that if he sprayed a handful of bullets at high velocity into the concrete driveway, one or two may go off. What fun! Bang-bang! Burp. Without a gun barrel the bullet parts will fly anywhere, but in Tom's world this is the joy of life's lottery to discover who, if anyone, is selected for hilarious contact, injury or death. In just a few minutes, slews of bullets are slammed into the concrete, all without success. Or perhaps *with* success, since no-one got shot. And then JR arrived.

It's a credit to Tom's honesty that he's such a bad liar; the way he tried to conceal the wrist-rocket behind his back was cartoonishly hopeless. JR immediately smelt a rat and asked what Tom was hiding. "Nothing" said Tom, absurdly, while reddening. When JR saw the catapult, his mind segued towards what was being fired. It wasn't the season for acorns, but drunken stupidity is not thus constrained. He scanned the ground. Right at his feet a few signature golden missiles sparkled up at him. That's when the shouting started.

"What the hell are you doing firing bullets in my driveway, Hostetler?! You ***!!"**

JR was giving thought to his daughter, then his only child. Now a statuesque teenager, Jessica was then barely two: padding around her world in wide-eyed wonder. Understandably, JR was not amused by the prospect of his beloved little girl toddling into the house with a mouthful of live ammunition just because Hostetler had recently paid a house-call.

As he ranted, I sensed impending doom; JR had only seen those few bullets. The inevitable moment came when his head turned and he saw, across his entire back yard, the scattered array of ordnance as far as the eye could see. His breath was arrested, his tirade stilled in the eye of the storm, as he goggled at the scale of the offence, while we stared stupidly down at our beer bottles.

And that's when the shouting *really* started.

Bullets and Beer

Attending a Gun Range – Tom's World (1998)

When Tom first invited me to go shooting I accepted enthusiastically. In England the average citizen won't encounter a gun at any point in their lifetime, so it sounded fun. We loaded up a .22 handgun, a small-bore rifle and a 30-30 Winchester, which dispenses both bullets and jaw-restructuring physiotherapy with a single pull, and headed out to the range.

But Tom's idea of a gun range differs from society's. He simply pulled over by the side of coastal Highway 1 and we tramped off into the hillside's long grass with the firearms and a stock of Newcastle Brown ale (I was still clinging to some English comforts). We entertained ourselves by setting up rocks at various distances and blowing them apart with the 30-30, all the while regaled by the ocean's gloriously salty aroma and seething hiss; pierced by the squawks of overhead gulls. We fired till the 'Nukes' were drunk and only once did Tom shoot while I was still setting up. In fairness, he hit the rock. Finally the beers were gone and there were holes in everything except us (we checked) so we deemed it a roaring success.

Attending a Gun Range – the Real World (1999)

However, when half a dozen of us went shooting together, convention prevailed and we went to a gun range on Skyline Boulevard & Highway 9 (off which Hostetler later launched his Miata). We had shotguns, semi-automatic rifles, handguns, clay pigeons, targets and much enjoyment. But where it all went rather pear-shaped was on the handgun range. Tom and I had wandered from the others and had this area to ourselves. Tom scrunched a Coke can he had fished out of a nearby trash can, lobbed it lazily over the guard rail, where it landed three feet away, and said: "There, chase that around."

I duly obliged. With the first shot the can sprang satisfyingly into the air with requisite cartoon 'ping' and 'p-yow' noises. But as I continued firing and the can danced away from its tormentor, a shouting steward bore down, much energized. It transpired one was not permitted to shoot at any object less than seven yards away, and no more than 25. Whitewashed lines declared the exact distances where grave recklessness magically transformed into safe entertainment. Tom stood silently by as I was reamed out, admitting no complicity, looking as innocent as a long-suffering grandfather. I absorbed the tirade solo, making a mental note to extract an appropriate beer debt later. "Behold The Wake," and so forth.

There was nothing to shoot at in the legal range except for a few cans in the far 25 yard distance which, like the steward's safety arguments, already bore too many holes to present a worthy target. Disenchanted, I merely handed the pistol to Tom. Tom gamely squeezed off a couple of rounds at the distant shrapnel and became instantly bored.

At this point a pigeon fatefully cooed in the trees behind. With no second thought, Tom's arm flew skywards and he shot into the canopy. Three, four slugs were jettisoned into the tree-line, though the bird had never been visible. I must admit I thought this was a tad offside myself. At some point those bullets were going to come down and the good citizens of Skyline Boulevard behind the trees, both residents and day hikers, might be irked by the shower of hot lead. Instinctively I glanced back at the steward. He had not retired far, as if sensing his day's work with us might not be done. His face was a curious contortion: simultaneously trying to clench his teeth and shout at the same time, which led to a comedic conflict over the control of his jaw. When he finally regained the power of speech he gave free rein to his emotions – via the purplest of prose, I might add – ensconced in which was the unmistakable invitation for us to depart. We haven't been back.

Once Upon a Tom

Party Like it's 1999

It was the summer of
'99. The Nasdaq boomed at its
all-time high. Spirits soared;
oblivious to the busts around
the corner. JR had obtained a
second property in Capitola, by
the beach, and was installing appliances.

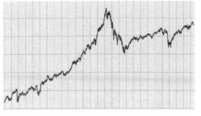

Figure 4.1: Nasdaq Index, 1985-
2012. The peak is summer 1999

The plan was simple. Washer, dryer and refrigerator are
tethered to a trailer and pulled by JR's Chevy Tahoe. His
perpetual nervousness required Tom to drive in convoy to watch
for potential load-shifts; and assist manhandling items into the
house. Typically, JR had bought a cooler of beer to reward Tom's
help. (Equally typically, it was cheap, awful beer.)

Signs of impending disaster came almost immediately.
Before they even set off, Tom was insisting on carrying the beer.
JR was suspicious, but relented, ordering the cooler placed in the
back of Tom's covered pick-up. Tom did, but snagged one
straight away for the ride. JR rolled his eyes and sighed.

They had travelled less than ten of the 50 miles when
Tom first disappeared. One minute he's reliably in JR's rear-view
mirror, the next, he's simply gone. And we can be sure JR was
checking the mirror every three seconds. JR pulled over on 85
southbound and waited. Two minutes later Tom's red truck
barrelled by and the convoy was reconnected. But it didn't last.
Five minutes later Tom had disappeared again. "What the hell?!"
JR muttered and, panicking that there's car trouble, pulled to the
side once more. As before, the red truck roared by a minute later.
But the third time Tom pulled over, on a precarious embankment
on Hwy 17, the mantle of mystery came unfastened. Tom is seen
scurrying to the back of the vehicle for a refill; indeed now he

simply hauls the whole beer cooler into the front of the truck. The previous stops have been beer breaks, not car trouble. In his car JR vents curses at Tom: loudly, passionately, but unheard.

The saga sails into Capitola, and JR now has more to fret about than shifting cargo. The red truck is veering into the centre of 41ˢᵗ Avenue's four-lane flow and Tom's left arm extends from the window. To jaw-dropping amazement, Tom tries to slap the oncoming cars. Three, four times, he swats playfully at the traffic. He misses each time, which is fortuitous since his hand would've exploded in a shower of bone splinters on impact, hitting solid steel at a relative velocity of ~60 mph. Landing in jail would also be a less-than-wonderful consequence, should a driver report his madness (although when JR related the tale to me his only outrage, hilariously, was that if Tom were arrested he wouldn't have anyone to help him get his fridge through the front door).

They finally arrived and tensions were unleashed. JR raged about Tom's antics and – perhaps more so – the loss of beer; while Tom, alighting from his truck, was only concerned with his overfull bladder; urgently bouncing from foot to foot as if his boots were on fire. Needless to say, despite the decibels, there wasn't a great deal of actual communication.

"**What the hell were you playing at? And what am I supposed to drink now? You ******!!**"

"**Open the door JR, I gotta pee! Open the door!**"

"**How much beer's left? That was for both of us!**"

"**Open the door, dammit, I gotta pee now!**"

"**You just stepped in the gutter. I don't want muddy footprints on my white carpets.**"

"**I gotta pee, JR, OPEN THE DOOR <u>NOW</u>!!**"

Which is how, as Tom pounded down the passageway hollering for a toilet, the muddy footprints came to be imprinted on the carpet; Tom's flourishing sign-off to his day's assistance.

Disco Inferno:
The House on Washington Ave[*]

Jenny, Tom's elder daughter, writes of their cabin:

*"Small," was about all mom could say about it. "Small and old,"
she added. I imagined the house feeling poorly for itself. "She's a rustic
knotty-pine cabin in the redwoods next to a trickling river- this is heaven!"
my dad mandated; and in 1988 we left our apartment on 5th Avenue in San
Francisco and moved. The house on Washington was rarely quiet. The door
was always unlocked, even when we were on vacation, and everyone knew that
the house was for everyone. One time mom brought home a homeless girl from
town, and she stayed with us for a few weeks. Friends called it home.*

Tom's house was still a party palace when I touched
down a decade later: with or without visitors. One day Tom came
to work with a gashed forehead, explaining that an experimental
hallucinogen had sent him into disco fever. He'd hurtled
uncontrolled around the cabin solo until a solid collision with the
uncompromising door-jam had, in his words, "poked a hole in
his bag." It was that kind of place.

*When we moved in, she was 32, resting atop nineteen stilts, until
the 7.2 earthquake of '89, then she was on eleven. Her floors creaked and
the wind came through the cracks. There was no insulation. The first winter
we walked around the house in woolen socks and flannel jammies. The second
winter a wood-burning stove was installed and it burned for three months
straight. In the canyon the sun rose three hours later and set three hours
earlier than at the apartment.*

But the wood-burning stove formed a fickle family friend.
On Fri 8th Mar 2013, it turned enemy. The grout on the chimney
stack gave out; and the stove exhaled hot smoke through the gaps
overnight. The house was quickly smoke-filled and ablaze. Emily

---

* Co-authored with Jenny Hostetler

awoke, rousing Tom (likely saving his life since he sleeps soundly enough to miss an airstrike). Tom ran outside to retrieve the hosepipe and promptly fell in a hole he'd dug as underfloor access and meant to refill; scarring his leg to the point of stitches. (Two days later we scoured the hospital in a vain, tedious search for his ever-escaping Hat. It was on Tom's bed when he got home.) The home escaped condemnation and was rebuilt, hampered only by myriad discoveries of illegal "improvements" Tom had made over the years.

Figure 4.2: 8th Mar 2013, the House on Washington Ave. Firefighters look stupidly overdressed in their masks, helmets and O_2 cylinders as they wait patiently for Tom, protected only by poncho and the inevitable Hat, to stop prancing about front and centre

Today, if I could be there now, I would sit on the deck with the cat. I would walk inside where everything smells like wood smoke and light a fire. I'd sit in the big green couch and look up at the rafters and appreciate the cobwebs Dad loves so much. I would open the window when the fire had overheated the small house and hear the river, and smell the rotting leaves and smoke. I would walk into the hallway of a kitchen and grab a dirty mug from the pile of dishes in the sink and wash it, fill it with coffee from the percolator, way too much creamer and sugar, and return to my spot on the big green sofa. Later I'd share a bottle of red with dad while we solved the philosophical problems of the world. I'd listen to Gus' poetry or latest song lyrics and be honestly impressed. I'd play backgammon with Emily, or just snooze with the cat as the firelight danced on the walls. I'd feel at home.

As well she should, since it's officially Jenny's cabin now. For the House on Washington Ave, a new chapter is opening...

Turning Sixt-E[†]

You may not have turned sixty yourself. But you probably know someone who has. I wonder if they had a celebration at all? A family get-together in one of their homes, perhaps; loved ones clustered around a table for communal dinner and the warmth of shared fellowship? Maybe a grandchild shepherded them to a favorite beauty spot, or treated to afternoon tea? That's just how these things go.

But for House Hostetler, time-honored traditions lie discarded in the ditch alongside a more rakishly blazed trail. For Tom's 60th birthday in 2002, daughter Emily took him to a rave. In Oakland. Tom, of course, considered this a splendid suggestion: he loves to party and, with his natural Exuberance Enhanced with Extra Energizers (you figure it out), Tom was apparently the star of the show.

I can only imagine him as the white-haired centerpiece of the crowd. I can almost see the cowboy-hat-topped, eye-glazed, grin-plastered, limb-wiggling goodness that propelled him to the top of the popularity charts that night. I wasn't there myself (clearly I'm not yet old enough to be taken to raves) but obviously Emily was and she it is who stewards the tantalizing details of this story.

Emily's bubbly helpfulness and fun-filled nature meant she was excited to contribute said details to this book too; yet that proved to be easier said than done. Her social calendar is more heavily populated than a Tokyo nightclub sporting all-night schoolgirl karaoke; and amidst all this, the timing coincided with both the house fire (as per the previous story) and her securing the enviable position of flight attendant, with its time-intensive training regimen and subsequent scant guaranteed free time at

---

† Co-authored with Emily Hostetler, Tom's younger daughter

any particular location. Emily and I tried to meet three times for me to extract the spicy details before she sallied forth on her professional city-hopping extravaganza, but the combination of this busyness and ambient confusion confounded each registered rendezvous.

Obtaining the details via online messaging also yielded less than total victory; here's a smattering of our attempts:

John Pople to Emily Hostetler, 31st Mar 2014, 4:51pm
> I imagine you're super-busy with [flight attendant] training, but you're still very welcome to send details of the rave for Tom's 60th birthday, or we can figure a time to Skype about it.

Emily Hostetler to John Pople, 31st Mar 2014, 5:12pm
> ☺

John Pople to Emily Hostetler, 8th Jun 2014, 8:33pm
> How's the 60th birthday story coming along? (Raw details are fine.) We need to hit print fairly soon; it takes a while to get an ISBN…

Emily Hostetler to John Pople, 8th Jun 2014, 9:02pm
> ☺

Sometimes, the apple simply doesn't fall all that far from the tree…

Dining Etiquette

Once during a medical consultation in 2007 I was asked if I ever drank alcohol during the week. I readily replied that a couple of drinks on a weekday was by no means unthinkable. The doctor, a firm teetotaler, tut-tutted primly.

"You really should try to find other activities after work."
"Oh no," I disclosed truthfully, "that's at lunch."
The shrewish doctor lost it. "**LUNCH?!!**" he shouted.

There was a sharp silence while he recovered himself. "I'm sorry," he said, "I didn't mean to yell: you took me by surprise." But he couldn't let the matter go. Minutes later while diagnosing he was still muttering: "Can't believe lunchtime drinking still happens!" and "This isn't the 1980s!" while shaking his head in disbelief. In the end his prescriptions included daily injections, presumably purely out of moral disgust.

Figure 4.3: Typical City Pub lunch, 2009: Tom, Scott Jansson and me. Tom would have raised his own glass had he not already finished it

As for the pub lunches themselves, Redwood City's own 'City Pub' was a frequent, favourite haunt. The staff were always gregarious, always generous and sometimes gorgeous; there was Guinness on tap and we could sit out in the sun. We were even allowed to bring Tom without a leash. Relevant to the story, City

Pub also has a decades long tradition of beer shots: 10 oz pours designed to be slammed, not sipped, which are wheeled out on occasions of salute, celebration or challenge.

One lunchtime Dave, Tom and I were reclining in liquid comfort as server and friend JR Bolton (not to be confused with co-worker JR Troxel) bustled past with the slop bucket. Without pausing to think, Tom nimbly dipped into the leftovers and snagged a tomato slice, which he gorged in a single mouthful. JR halted in mid-stride; equal parts amused and revolted, not sure whether to believe what he had just seen. I buried my face in my hands while Dave stared hard enough at Tom to cause injury.

"Dude, you only have to ask and I'll bring you a whole *side* of tomato," offered JR. Tom waved his hand airily. "No need," he blathered magnanimously, "that was just right."

Not two minutes later, JR returned to our table bearing two Guinness shots. Tom, by now revelling in the infamy, rose to the challenge, literally, and stood alongside JR.

I'd never seen JR lose a beer shot before.

But Tom was simply on fire that day: the Guinness couldn't have gone down any faster if he'd thrown the glass clean over his shoulder. Our disapproving glares were replaced with goggling surprise. Male bar staff at City Pub generally hone their beer-shot prowess studiously, JR as successfully as any, and they take great care not to lose (while taking even greater care to look as if they're not taking any care at all). Losing a beer shot to a 69 year-old man who dines from the slop bucket has got to be an interesting addition to any barman's résumé.

If nothing else, Tom never loses his capacity to surprise. Did anyone mention a box of chocolates?

Once Upon a Tom
'SLAC Today' Article

This book is the first comprehensive assembly of Tom-stories, but some have sneaked out before, at least in preview form. The article below, from 2009, is a spoof on SLAC's site-wide magazine: SLAC Today, which features staff achievements. By now you'll be familiar with many of the individual Tom stories which the article and its footnotes obliquely reference…

SLAC today

People: Stanford Welcomes New Emeritus Professor at SLAC
by James Frey

20 Mar 2009

I had the privilege to interview Stanford's newest Emeritus chair: Thomas E. Hostetler, of Stanford's Synchrotron Radiation Lightsource. I was aware that Prof. Hostetler was a prodigious writer and had published both books and papers on a wide range of topics, including: "**I Swallowed an Oleander**: Creative Highway Maneuvers," (2001, John Wiley & Sons); "**Interesting Flora and Fauna I Found On My Shoe**," (2002, Harper-Collins); and "**Splashy, Splashy**: Protocols for Handling Liquid Nitrogen in US National Laboratories" (2008, SLAC-PUB-10972, Stanford).

Thomas E Hostetler. (File Photo; courtesy SLAC Hum. Res. Dept.)

I caught up with Prof Hostetler in the SSRL parking lot, picking shards of a MADD placard out of his front grill. He invited me to his office where we could discuss his appointment.

"What contribution to the scientific community do you think was principal in your securing this position?" I asked as I trailed behind his casual stride.

"I'm not sure," he replied modestly, belching and tripping on the stairs, "but possibly it was my research on determining the native state of arsenic." I was familiar with the work: a year-long effort that had impacted the arenas of scientific discovery[1] and professional communications.[2]

The office itself was testament to the breadth of Prof Hostetler's study. Dog-eared textbooks on both physics and philosophy were equally to hand, amidst half-constructed electrical gizmos, vacuum glassware, prosthetic limbs and the occasional discarded fig roll.

Prof Hostetler says: "Stop the Madness!"

Disconcertingly, there were clearly areas of movement amidst the debris.

[1] J. L. Frink: "**Professor Frink's Almanac of Frivolous Inquiry**," 2009, Penguin Books, pp 272-5
[2] T. E. Hostetler, "**Please Indulge My Groping**: A Buffoon's Guide to Interdepartmental Memos," 2009, SLAC-PUB-11313, Stanford

Party On, Wayne

This article was printed on a lazy Friday afternoon, to release the pressure of a particularly rough week navigating The Wake. But whether it was natural justice, or simply poor fortune, there was barely a soul to be found on the synchrotron floor with whom I could share my evil concoction. Dave and JR were both there; but beyond that I delivered copies to the mailboxes of those I knew would understand, and sloped off for the weekend.

SLAC today

Prof Hostetler performing electrical safety testing. The fact he was not flung ten yards to finish up against a dumpster with his hat on fire led him to conclude there was no compromise of the electric ground.

Prof Hostetler offered me a seat, so I swept the squirrel droppings off the nearest chair and sat down. It was an intimidating scene: many physics equations in Prof Hostetler's own hand adorned the whiteboard, bearing the remarkable indication that Newton, Maxwell and Einstein had all been significantly astray in their thinking.

"What have been your favorite activities over the years at SSRL?" I wanted to know.

"A little of everything, really," he replied, waving airily and knocking a pint of cold coffee into my lap. This claim is readily corroborated by his co-workers, J.R. Troxel and D. Day, who scowled and said he had 'more fingers in more pies than a leper on a cookery course.'

"I've always enjoyed the pleasure and challenge of user support,"[3] he continued, "and the collaborative spirit in this laboratory of being able to pursue my own research in conjunction with some of the finest minds in academia.[4] I'm privileged to see some of my theories recorded in the literature,[5] and I'm grateful to my former mentors, especially Hal Tompkins, for encouraging me in all

Prof Hostetler arrives early for his inauguration ceremony at the Stanford Dean's residence

these endeavors." When I caught up with Dr. Tompkins for response, he returned a withering stare and said: "Keep him the hell away from LCLS."

Nevertheless, through it all, we can rest assured that, as the wheels of research science continue their inexorable revolution, somewhere, somehow, Prof. Thomas E. Hostetler is trying very hard to be helpful. Bravo Tom!

[3] "**Stop it! Stop it! Stop it!**: Assisting the Ungrateful User," Rev. Sci. Instrum., 2004, Vol. 3, pp 364-9
[4] T. E. Hostetler, "**Watch This! Bzzzzt!**: Fondly Remembering Former Colleagues," 2009, Zondervan
[5] N. G. McWhirter, "**Guinness Book of Wild Drunken Assertions**," 2009, MacMillan, pp 170-202

In the end, it's not the years in your life that count.
It's the life in your years.

Abraham Lincoln

...and Last

Still Having Fun

Tom is fun. And being a fun person can't be faked. In fact, Tom foghorns his fun so clearly that total strangers are immediately intoxicated by his aura. I'm not in the slightest surprised that the San Jose Mercury reporter described SSRL as a "**toy store of science**" when toured by Tom.[1] Independently harmonizing, the SLAC Today journalist who interviewed Tom for her article (a real SLAC Today article on Tom exists as well as the preceding spoof) knew to entitle her piece: "**Tom Hostetler is Still Having Fun**,"[2] from which this closing section's title is taken. To the outside observer both pieces may seem to have rare, unlikely headings. For Tom's friends, we know nothing else could have sufficed.

For Tom, fun is not only ready relaxation in the Earth's luxuries that flash upon his inward eye so easily, but also the active sampling of new information and experiences. Only the other day he asked me: "When the eye is relaxed, is the pupil contracted or dilated?" From anyone else it would be a bizarre enquiry (seriously, who thinks to ask that? – or care?!). But from Tom it was par for the course. By reflex I fixed the studiously straight face of one who was appropriately informed and told him it depended on whether you were left or right-handed, just to wickedly revel in his frustrated grimace.

Tom leaves no stone unturned in his quest to grasp the universe more closely. He has ransacked the sacred pockets of Christianity, Zen-Buddhism, Freemasonry and philosophy; he has rattled the very bars of Heaven to find out who's home. He has

---

[1] N Gonzalez, "Students visit toy store of science," San Jose Mercury News 06 Dec 2007, http://www.mercurynews.com/ci_7649057

[2] C. Cofield, "Tom Hostetler is Still Having Fun," SLAC Today 03 Dec 2008, http://today.slac.stanford.edu/feature/2008/profile-hostetler.asp

even tried to understand cricket. Yet in each of these journeys the inimitable essence of Tom remains. His journey into Christianity, for example, was prompted by an acid trip while riding a bicycle, which I somehow doubt is the canonical procedure for admission into either seminary or ministry. Yet it neatly iconizes how, for all Tom hurls himself into every new immersion to willingly achieve any available metamorphosis, his essential kernel persists.

Jenny confirms:

Tom has always been distinctly Tom. When he was in the Christian Community in San Francisco, he was baptized three times. When my mom was baptized she was renamed, as was the custom, from Beatrice to Joanna. Each time Tom was baptized the clergyman made the appropriate ceremonies and crosses in the air over his head, and all three times came out with 'Tom,' 'Tom,' and 'Tom.'

(It occurs to me that the clergyman may have been communicating that he was well out of his depth to hope to change Tom and could he please be relieved now?)

Tom does not limit his pursuit of enjoyment to himself, either: his desire to share is innate. For his children he created grandiose arcana to give dimension to even a humble mantle ornament.

Jenny reveals:

In his cowboy days in Arizona… he stumbled upon a dragon in one of the caves. He and the dragon talked and came to the conclusion that either one of them or both might die if it came to blows. The dragon agreed at gunpoint to be shrunk and frozen for one hundred years, plenty of time for Tom to grow old and die. Unfortunately it wasn't necessarily plenty of time for his kids to grow old and die, what with life expectancy on the rise and all. Three years later I was born and at around eight I started to worry about what to do with this miniature dragon, which sat on the mantelpiece of the fireplace and looked down on me with an evil grin. I would be ninety-seven when he awoke, and what about my children, and grandchildren?

A case in point: one weekend I found myself without a car, so Tom, ever generous, lent me one of his. It's churlish to look a gift horse in the mouth, so forgive me for checking the trunk before driving away, but this caution was purely a product of long Wake-surfing experience. Having so done, I invited Tom to continue as steward of both the rifle and the bag of famously enjoyable herbs that languished therein. "Oh there it is!" Tom exclaimed in unalloyed delight at the discovery of the latter, which had apparently been missing for weeks. Happily, we had assisted each other.

This deeply held appreciation of fun, combined with an easy generosity, cornerstone Tom's sociability. The above stories may suggest Tom's co-workers are permanently roaring threats of retribution and waving frustrated fists at his retreating form as he strides carelessly into the sunset and we are left helplessly bobbing in The Wake once more; but in reality Tom is hugely popular with us all. JR exemplifies:

You can't help but love Tom. I love working with him (he's always trying very hard to be helpful) because he has a way about him where he can sense when you need assistance. I love listening to Tom: he can cover all subjects eloquently — whether it be about personal matters, science or even Zen. My favorite time with Tom had to be his personally guided tour of the USS Pampanito (a similar vessel to the one on which Tom served his time in the Navy). He was like a kid in a candy store, excitedly pointing out all the sub's features. I truly enjoy hanging out with Tom anywhere: at work, a ball-game, SemiCon West [3] or most of all just enjoying a cold one.

Likewise Dave echoes:

I have worked with Tom for approximately 25 years. Even though the stories that are told are true he really has been fun to work with. I may have not agreed on some of his methods, but we came away unscathed. Tom is always the first to try very hard to be helpful, even when help is not needed, but that is the kind of person Tom is. Tom has been a good friend throughout the years and has been a huge part of the SSRL family. I will really miss Tom; even though we joke about who is going to be the 'work-maker' after he retires. Who loves you baby?

And for myself, perhaps I have gained most of all. For more than a decade Tom and I went to lunch together almost every day and discussed everything under – and above – the sun. I suppose I should first have mentioned that he was the principal technician who worked alongside me restoring the Materials Science small-angle x-ray scattering (SAXS) program on SSRL's Beamline 1-4, which indeed he was, but in truth it was the lunchtimes that were more important. No other one person has shaped my own abilities to reason and reflect quite so profoundly. And every discussion, however intellectual, philosophical or spiritual, was also, always, fun.

The lunchtimes themselves were florid affairs. We drenched ourselves in sunshine and fraternity at many a roadside café, lightly sautéed in the *vino du jour*, as horses plodded lugubriously under shady boughs and insects buzzed and zipped

---

[3] SemiCon West is an annual Northern California microelectronics conference focused on semi-conductor equipment, processes and materials. Under no circumstances should it be understood to be a blatant boondoggle into fun-filled San Francisco stuffed with food, beer, pool, cocktails and slurred camaraderie as staff rampage wantonly through the city.

breathlessly amid unkempt stalks. California's near-eternal summer is truly a glorious thing. The bucolic ambience was vulnerable only to rumbling concrete trucks, when we covered our glasses with maternal protection and spluttered away the blankets of spiraling dust. Friendly servers were inexorably lured into our company, piqued by the frisson of debate and banter pervading our lunchtime milieu. And they helped clear up a lot of the spillages, too. Yet I'm under no illusions as to who was the star of the show. Perchance I would lunch alone, I might be accosted with: "Where's your friend?" (or sometimes: "Where's your crazy friend?") in a slightly hurt tone, as if I had committed some misdemeanor just to have the temerity to turn up without him. There was little doubt I was only the straight man of our comedy duo; depending on your age and culture I was the Abbott to his Costello, the Ernie to his Eric, the Teller to his Penn.

This is Tom's legacy to SSRL (and perhaps in time to all of us): The Man who Knew How to Have Fun. An iconic scene he leaves SSRL is the paper blow-darts he shot into the insulation panels of the synchrotron building's roof, 30 feet above the beamline floor, by Beamline 1. I'm privileged that the most recent dart was fired there solely for my benefit in '98, since I couldn't believe it could be done with only paper. Apparently it could. As often, Tom was right and my scepticism was amiss.

Ultimately, how shall any of us be remembered? Perhaps it's an issue we mentally postpone, as long as we're not staring eyeball to eye-socket with the scythe-wielding specter. But it impinges nonetheless. At SSRL I may be remembered as the minister-posing-as-physicist who happily hosted all friends wandering by (Tom nicknamed my tiny home-made office "The Confessional"); or maybe the beamline scientist who extended lunchtime to *Hitch Hikers Guide to the Galaxy* proportions. To be remembered as the guy who is "Still Having Fun" is a gold-medal accolade for sure; and that podium is occupied.

What would be the highest prize? Could we hope to be remembered as one so generous as to assist all others' logistical and financial needs; so philosophical as to genuinely explore all thought-trains well beyond our cultural experience; so Christian as to bear all unwarranted wounds without complaint (in Tom's case, many from the irate verbal savagery of yours truly) and yet, despite it all, be so changed and unchanged to greet us again each morning with unfeigned and unfettered joy?

Logic's verdict is unwavering: such a man cannot exist.

Yet, for all I feel like a man reporting a Big-Foot sighting, I think I did meet a man like this once; if only once. Once upon a time.

Once upon a Tom.

1996 [1]

2014 [2]

---

[1] Courtesy, Emily Hostetler
[2] © 2014 Jen Hostetler Photography. Used with permission

"From my rotting body, flowers shall grow
and I am in them, and that is eternity"
Edvard Munch

If you enjoyed this book, find it on lulu.com and leave a happy review!
If you hated this book, burden someone you don't like with your copy and tell
them it's a must-read